IF GOD IS GOD THEN WHY?

Letters from New York City

AL TRUESDALE

Beacon Hill Press of Kansas City
Kansas City, Missouri

10 9 8 7 6 5 4 3 2 1

For all who suffer

Note to the Reader

The persons and letters that compose this book are fictional. The book is written with deep sensitivity to and respect for those who were killed or injured, and for those who suffered the injuries and deaths of loved ones and friends, in the September 11, 2001, attack in New York City, Washington, D.C., and Pennsylvania. Hopefully, making the New York City tragedy the book's setting will expose something of the depth of moral evil, the magnitude of human suffering, and the meaning of Christian hope. I hope that the book will lead the honest questioner to the God who suffers with us in Christ.

The Lament

On Friday, September 14, 2001, United States President George W. Bush spoke the following words during a National Day of Prayer service at the National Cathedral in Washington, D.C.:

We are here in the middle hour of our grief. So many have suffered so great a loss, and today we express our nation's sorrow. We come before God to pray for the missing and the dead, and for those who loved them.

On Tuesday, our country was attacked with deliberate and massive cruelty. We have seen the images of fire and ashes and bent steel. Now come the names, the list of casualties we are only beginning to read.

They are the names of men and women who began their day at a desk or in an airport busy with life. They are the names of people who faced death and in their last moments called home to say, "Be brave" and "I love you." They are the names of passengers who defied their murderers and prevented the murder of others on the ground. They are the names of men and women who wore the uniform of the United States and died at their posts. They are the names of rescuers, the ones whom death found running up the stairs and into the fires to help others.

What national tragedy, what horrible chain of events, could possibly have called forth such somber and anguished words? The answer: the bloodiest day on American soil since the Civil War.

The Deed

At 7:59 A.M. September 11, 2001, American Airlines Flight 11 to Los Angeles lifted off from Logan International Airport in Boston. Captain John Ogonowski, who lived on a farm north of the city, was piloting the aircraft, which carried 9 flight attendants and 81 passengers. Flight 11 fell mysteriously silent. The air traffic controller called over and over for a response. None came. Then he heard an unidentified voice from the cockpit: "We have some planes. Just stay quiet, and you'll be OK. We . . ."

Shortly before 8:45 A.M. Flight 11, flying at an altitude of 900 feet, directly approached the silvery twin towers of the World Trade Center on the tip of Manhattan.

At 8:46 A.M., as dozens of businessmen, members of the exclusive World Trade Center Club, enjoyed a leisurely breakfast and the spectacular view on the 107th floor, Flight 11 slammed into the north tower 20 floors below. Most people on the ground thought there had been a sonic boom or a construction accident. But as the gruesome "rains" —bits of plane, a tire, office furniture, glass, a hand, a leg, whole bodies—began falling all around, people in the streets stopped and stared, falling silent.

The plane had been hijacked by terrorists and was under the control of the hijackers.

Dead: all on board.

At 7:58 A.M. United's Flight 175 also left its gate at Logan International Airport in Boston. With 56 persons aboard, the wheels of the Boeing 767 were in the air by 8:15 A.M. Victor J. Saracini, 50, an experienced pilot, was at the controls. At some point, men armed with knives stabbed flight attendants. A cell phone caller on the plane gave the details in several brief calls to his father in Connecticut. Until 8:47 A.M. the flight was on course heading toward Los Angeles. Then it made a sharp left turn.

At 9:03 A.M., while the attention of the world was riveted on the already damaged north tower of the World Trade Center, its engines screaming, Flight 175 plowed into the south tower. Loaded with fuel for a transcontinental flight, it exploded into a massive fireball that instantly engulfed the upper levels of the building. The plane's approach and impact were homicidal and theatrical. The planners of the carnage must have known the murderous scene would be broadcast everywhere.

By force of the impact and the firestorm that burst from the exploding fuel, people, desks, and chairs were sucked out the windows, raining down onto the streets below. Police officers, firefighters, and pedestrians watched and wept. As the fire and debris fell, cars exploded. The air smelled of smoke and concrete.

Fanatical terrorists were in control of Flight 175 when it crashed into the south tower and exploded.

Dead: all on board.

At approximately 8:11 A.M. American Airlines Flight 77, a twin engine 757, left Dulles International Airport near Washington, D.C., bound for Los Angeles. Most of its seats were empty. The people who sat near windows had a beautiful view of the Blue Ridge Mountains and then the Ohio River Valley far below. Among the 58 passengers was a group of schoolchildren on a National Geographic field trip. There were three 11-year-olds, three teachers from Washington public schools, and two National Geographic Society officials. Also present was the president of a California company that helped employees balance their work and personal lives. But several hijackers with knives were also aboard.

Shortly after 8:51 A.M. Flight 77 turned around and began to make a 300-mile trip back east. The hijackers had turned the plane into a lethal missile, the intended target of which is still uncertain. Many think the target might have been the White House.

As Flight 77 turned back toward Washington, the two other planes had already hit both towers of the World Trade Center, which were now in flames. Even as Flight 77 bore down on Washington, officials knew that the plane had been hijacked and was now embarked upon a murderous mission. The passengers had been herded into the rear of the plane. The pilot was with them—not in the cockpit.

As the fuel-laden missile bore down on Washington, it crossed the Potomac River and slammed into the Pentagon. The time was 9:45 A.M.

Dead: The Pentagon announced on Thursday, September 14, that 125 service members and civilians were missing and presumed dead. This report raised the death toll at the Pentagon to 189, including the 64 passengers and crew members aboard Flight 77.

By 8:44 A.M. United Flight 93, bound for San Francisco, lifted off from Newark, New Jersey. The plane headed west and apparently flew without incident until it approached Cleveland, about 50 minutes into the flight.

At 9:37 A.M. the plane turned south and headed back the way it had come. In a series of cellular telephone calls to their wives, two passengers gave harrowing details of the hijacking now in progress. To keep others from dying even if they could not save themselves, they vowed to try to overcome the enemy. The men joked about taking on the hijackers by using the butter knives from the in-flight breakfast.

At approximately 10:10 A.M., as the rogue plane soared over woodlands, pastures, and cornfields, it passed over Kelly Leverknight's home. It then smashed into a reclaimed section of a strip mine near Somerset, Pennsylvania.

Dead: All on board. A total of 266 persons on the four planes had died that day.

Back in New York City, the burning towers, still containing thousands of persons, were about to turn to powder. Steel starts to bend at 1,000 degrees F. In the south tower, the floors above the plane's impact were resting on steel now softening from the heat of burning jet fuel. Each floor weighed millions of pounds. The girders softened until they could no longer bear the load above. As the steel bent, the structure became untenable. The weight bore down on floors that were not designed to bear it. The collapse began.

Each floor dropped onto the one below. The weight became greater and greater. Eventually the entire building came straight down, each floor pancaking down, trapping thousands of persons between the floors on the way down. The south tower collapsed at 9:59 A.M. The north tower came down 29 minutes later. The mighty skyscrapers had been reduced to jagged stumps.

The Bitter Toll

In a "hellish storm of ash, glass, smoke and leaping victims," being devoured by flames, both towers of the World Trade Center had toppled to the ground in massive rushes that left a world horrified and speechless. The steel moaned, said Fannie Gibbs, and the cracks "spread in zippers through the walls" (Fannie Gibbs, "Special Report: The Day of the Attack," time.com, September 12, 2001). The 110-story structures came crashing down upon more than 3,000 fleeing occupants trying to rush down the stairs and those who were trapped and thus could not flee. Others on the upper floors had been seen leaping to their deaths rather than face death by fire.

The collapse quickly left smoldering, stories-high piles of rubble in place of the majestic towers. Ten hours later, the collapse of the towers caused another World Trade Center building to fall. According to one emergency medical technician who arrived early at the scene, as the towers collapsed, the debris picked people up and slammed them into buildings (*Time*, September 24, 2001, 70). Several other buildings in the area were damaged or aflame.

As the occupants were rushing down the stairs, firefighters, police officers, and other rescue workers who had responded to the first impact were struggling up the stairs through the smoke to rescue those trapped in the burning buildings. When the towers collapsed, over 350 New York City firefighters and 50 New York City police officers died. Hundreds more were treated for cuts, broken bones, burns, and smoke inhalation.

The attacks were carefully planned. All the hijacked planes were en route to California, gorged with fuel. Their departures had been careful spaced within an hour and 40 minutes. No one immediately claimed responsibility for the attacks. But the magnitude and sophistication of the scheme, the extensive planning required for coordinated hijackings by terrorists who had to be familiar with the planes they commandeered, and the history of major attacks on American targets in recent years led many officials and experts to point to Osama bin Laden, the Islamic militant thought to operate out of Afghanistan. By the end of the first week, as evidence mounted, even President Bush had publicly identified Osama bin Laden as the mastermind behind the carnage.

By Friday, September 15, the list of the missing stood at 4,717. As late as September 21 only five victims had been rescued alive. Two young women at Pennsylvania Station, awaiting a predawn train to Trenton, spotted a construction worker and two Philadelphia firefighters coated in grime. They were headed home after assisting at the disaster site.

"Lot of bodies?" one woman asked the construction worker.

"Body parts," he replied.

On Friday, September 15, *New York Times* reporter Susan Sachs described the scene in words that gave those who looked on from afar some idea of the horror and destruction the terrorists had visited upon an unsuspecting nation:

> Swarming with volunteers and soaked through by a chilly rain, the area of the World Trade Center disaster has become a muddy, malodorous and frenetic village built around shifting mounds of debris that, yesterday, yielded only the dead.
>
> Throughout the day, a steady trickle of firefighters and rescue workers carried body bags from the piles of wreckage to refrigerated trucks that were parked in several places around the 16-acre site.
>
> One worker who had tunneled into the debris said he had found the remains of people strapped into what seemed to be airplane seats. Another, in one of the most searing discoveries among the ruins, found the body of a flight attendant, her hands bound (Susan Sachs, "Heart-Rending Discoveries as Digging Continues in Lower Manhattan," *New York Times*, New York Region, September 15, 2001).

For the next two weeks rescuers combed through mountains of rubble in a grim search for survivors among the thousands presumed dead.

President Bush called for a national day of prayer and remembrance on Friday, September 14. Inspiring and solemn services of prayer occurred in houses of worship all across America. It was also observed, apparently spontaneously, in Britain, France, Italy, Israel, and other countries closely allied with the United States. Traffic halted, classes stopped, and people stood silent for three minutes all across Europe.

For days relatives and friends of the missing wandered lower Manhattan carrying pictures of those they sought. They hoped that someone might have seen them alive. Many others simply carried their loved ones in their hearts, hoping against hope that the grim predictions would prove wrong. In the days that followed, the horrible magnitude of the destruction clarified. Hospitals that had geared up to receive large numbers of injured began to lack for patients. No survivors were found in the tangle of concrete and steel. Still, an army of heroic volunteers searched, hoping that some survivors might be found.

One Story

Before the south tower came down, Eddie Priest*, 55, a commercial real estate broker with an office on the 88th floor, repeatedly called his daughter, Janice, to tell her that he was OK but that he was trapped. There was no place to go, no way to exit his floor, even though the building was about to plunge to its destruction. Speaking calmly at first, Eddie told his daughter of his love for her. But after a couple of calls, his voice grew strained. He must have known death was imminent.

Six months earlier, Janice's mother had died of ovarian cancer. She and her father had always been close. But since the death of Mrs. Priest, Janice and her father had grown even closer.

Larry Perez, Janice's husband, was one of New York City's bravest—a firefighter. He was among the firefighters in the south tower at 9:59 A.M. when it collapsed. He had gone in at 9:00 A.M. as a member of a squad of six firefighters trained for such emergencies. Larry and Janice had been married nine years. They had two children: Michelle, 7, and Tony, 4.

Larry and Janice were new Christians and had joined a church in New Jersey. They had been learning to pray together as a family. Larry had seemed to advance in his faith more quickly than Janice. Given to serious reflection and questions, Janice seemed to examine things more intensely than did Larry. Since childhood, Janice had been plagued by the injustices she saw in the world about her. In her early teens she concentrated her attention on the suffering of children. As a new Christian, Janice was having a difficult time reconciling the enormous evils in the world with all she was being taught about God's love.

Since September 11 Janice's faith has been taking a severe pounding. In addition to her personal grief over the loss of her father and husband, she is horrified by the unfathomable evil a few highly dedicated fanatics visited upon so many innocent people. The accumulating numbers of fatalities only compounds her perplexity and grief.

Barbara Middleton is a close friend of Larry and Janice. She was responsible for leading them to faith in Christ. Barbara is a professor of literature in a New Jersey community college. Although Barbara has been in New Jersey for much of her professional life, as the following letters show, she was raised in the Lowcountry of South Carolina and still retains a love for the region and the literature of the South.

Janice and Barbara's agonizing struggle with the reality of moral evil was candidly recorded in a series of letters Barbara wrote to an uncle living in Charleston, South Carolina. Barbara's Uncle Carl is a retired Episcopal priest who has served as both a parish minister and a part-time professor of theology in an Episcopal seminary.

Totally lacking in guile and driven by brutal honesty, Barbara asks the tough questions that threaten to overwhelm Janice's fragile faith. The letters give clarity to a torrent of questions tumbling from grieving Janice. But in many instances it's impossible to determine whether Barbara is speaking for Janice or for herself. Often she simply speaks for both of them.

The letters offer no superficial solutions. Uncle Carl is willing to stay with the conversation, although at times it seems that he and God are getting the worst of it. Clearly, Uncle Carl has no interest in defending God by trivializing evil.

These letters may be helpful to Christians who struggle to reconcile their faith in God with the multiple moral evils they encounter through their families and friends or learn of through the media. They will be of little interest to those for whom everything is already "tidy." Perhaps they will offer hope to those who, while enduring their own publicized tragedies, have protested, "If God *is* God, then this shouldn't have happened—this just shouldn't have happened."

*The story is compiled from numerous accounts. Names have been changed.

The Letters

1

Friday, September 14, 2001
New York City

Dear Uncle Carl,

Your telephone call to me on Wednesday afternoon has been one of the few stabilizing influences in my life since the attack on Tuesday. The entire city and nation are in horrified shock. In the past four days the lives of many people seem to have spun out of control. As I told you, Janice's father, Eddie, was in the south tower when the attack occurred. Her husband, Larry, a New York City firefighter, was one of the first called to the scene. Both Eddie and Larry are among the missing.

Janice is certain that her father is dead. But she hopes desperately that Larry will be found alive. She is horrified over the prospects of losing them both. And so am I. You will remember that 6 months ago Janice's mother, Miriam, died of ovarian cancer.

Uncle Carl, in the last 15 minutes before the Trade Center collapsed, Janice talked with her father three times. He tried to joke about how he knew he should have never gotten into real estate. They laughed together, but between his attempts to soften the reality with humor, he repeatedly told Janice he loved her, and the rising panic in his voice betrayed his fear of the impending disaster.

We have been told repeatedly by the New York City Fire Department that many people escaped the buildings before they collapsed. We want so much to believe Larry was one of those! Perhaps your newspaper carried the pictures of people jumping from the burning buildings, choosing to die from the fall instead of the fire. Thousands of innocent people bore the brunt of this terrorist attack against the United States, just as innocent people around the world are bearing the brunt of wars for which they are not responsible! It seems that evil usually targets the innocent.

I mentioned that Eddie and Janice had laughed together. Laughter was only beginning to return to their lives. Janice's mom's losing battle with ovarian cancer and the long journey through alternating hope and despair had ravaged Janice's spirit. Eddie, Larry, and her kids were Janice's reason to go on living. Now she is struggling to "keep it together" for her kids. How can a kindergartner and pre-school child understand the sudden loss of so much family? And how does Janice go on being the mother her children need with the grief that surrounds her?

Surely Larry will be found alive. Out of frustration and fear, Janice went to Larry's station to find out if he had been located. Disappointed, she returned empty-handed.

You asked about the condition of Janice's faith. I could sense anxiety in your voice, and for good reason. Janice is the first person I have led to Christ. So far, her faith has made appreciable progress, but it has experienced numerous bumps along the way. Janice embraces her new faith but has some deep, unresolved questions.

Janice and Larry have regularly attended church services with me, and she has become part of a discipleship group. She has confided in me several times that she wished she had the faith Larry had. "He accepts God's love so readily," she once told me. "Why can't I be more like that?" She is learning to read and study the Bible and is trying to keep up with the books you continue to send her.

But, Uncle Carl, since Tuesday the gruesome magnitude of the attacks has begun to settle in. Janice has been forced to face the possibility that both Eddie and Larry might be dead, and her faith is suffering noticeably. To tell the truth, mine isn't hitting on all eight cylinders either.

As Janice told you when you were here in March, for years she dismissed the Christian faith. Her principal reason was the reality of evil. She found it incomprehensible that a good God and evil could exist in the same world. Truthfully, I had never given much attention to the problem evil poses for faith. Not that I had resolved anything; I suppose I just hadn't thought much about it.

This has certainly not been true for Janice. As I have tried to answer her sincere questions, I have been forced to confront the triviality of my own "solutions."

Since Tuesday, Janice's plaguing questions have come storming back with vengeance. Her attempts to pray lie littered about her.

Janice certainly doesn't think that New York City is an island of suffering or that her grief should receive special attention. She grieves for those killed in Washington and Pennsylvania. And she is profoundly aware of the occurrence of monstrous evils elsewhere in the world. The slave trade in Sudan and the many AIDS orphans in Africa have been particularly disturbing. In fact, it is the relentlessness and universality of moral evil that weighs so heavily upon her. And you can imagine that for her own children Janice is having a difficult time explaining why their grandfather and father are no longer here for them.

Recently Janice showed to me a statement by Zbigniew Brzezinski, former assistant to the president for national security affairs. He said that between 1914 and 1997, wars have killed 197 million people. That number is equivalent to nearly 1 in 20 of the total world population in 1990, or roughly the entire population of the United States in 1970.

Uncle Carl, either Janice will have to receive some honest and intelligible answers to her questions, or she will very likely say "Farewell!" to her faith. Recently when she tried to ask questions in a Bible study group, she was told that her doubts prove that she "doesn't love Jesus." I remember when my responses would not have been much better.

References to "miracles" abound in the aftermath of the September 11 attack. Yesterday I saw in the paper a story of one couple whose 33-year-old son worked in the Trade Center. The distraught father said, "We are praying for a miracle." I have heard the story of a man, somewhere near the 80th floor when one of the buildings collapsed, who "rode the wreckage" as the building fell. He was taken away from the scene with merely a broken leg. Some Christians have been quick to identify the narrow escape as a "divine miracle." I spoke with a secretary in a brokerage firm who overslept on the morning of the 11th. Had she made it to work on time, she would likely have been in the south tower when United Flight 175 struck it. The person is now telling anyone who will listen that God intervened and caused her to oversleep. She is certain that God saved her life and seems to have no sense of the broader implications of her statements. Janice and I have heard numerous similar shortsighted claims. Janice wonders why God could not have placed a deep sleep over a few thousand more people who did arrive at work on time.

Reports of such "divine intervention" disturb Janice. She says they remind her of a situation in which an adult who is supposed to be supervising a small child carelessly allows her to ride a tricycle into the street. An oncoming car strikes and mangles the child's body. Immediately, the careless adult rushes out of the house and into the street to begin caring for the child's wounds, trying to make her comfortable, attempting to stop the bleeding.

Some people say the adult is blameworthy because of carelessness. But then friends quickly rise to defend. They say that the critics are most unfair to concentrate on the adult's "apparent carelessness." Instead, the critics should praise and honor the person for the excellent care given to the child after the accident. Beyond doubt, the defenders say, this service to the wounded child proved the adult's love and responsibility.

Janice says that no one in his or her right mind would believe such a defense. But all over the country people are being asked to accept just such a defense for a God who is supposed to be all-powerful and all-loving. The illogic in this defense of God and the implications regarding His timing and justice have caused Janice to ask, "Is this what it takes to prop up God and substantiate one's faith? If so, don't be surprised if honest and thoughtful people (including me) 'check out'!"

Uncle Carl, I will not belittle Janice's crisis of faith. She will likely not go farther until some good answers are forthcoming. In an effort to explain why God might have allowed the attack, some ministers have given bizarre explanations. Their "answers" cheapen the lives of the victims and their families. And they don't do God much of a favor either. One minister tried to compare the Trade Centers to a modern-day Tower of Babel. "By its quick removal," the reverend said, "God is declaring the transience of man and his accomplishments." Apparently the minister missed the point that God didn't kill those who built the Tower of Babel and that the goal for building the Trade Centers was neither part of man's "quest for immortality" nor an effort to defy God.

On the one hand, we are being assured that when the attacks occurred, God wasn't in the vicinity. On the other hand, we are being urged to put our trust in God because "He loves us and will protect us." Janice wants to know, and I suppose I do, too, "Which one is it?" "Why," she has asked me, "should we worship such a truant?" This morning as I was preparing breakfast for her, she asked, "Must a person reject basic logic in order to be a Christian?"

Uncle Carl, I can't adequately answer Janice's questions. Will you help? Clearly, Janice intends to "have it out with God." If such language is too offensive, then she at least intends to "have it out with the problem of evil." Will God hear her out?

As you know, through the years I have respected your faith and honesty. Some of my fondest memories stem from the times you and I sat at night on the Charleston Battery in front of Rainbow Row. As we let the Atlantic breezes sweep over us, we talked of many things. You would talk about the meaning of Christ's call to discipleship, and you never dodged my questions.

Will you let me direct Janice's (and my) questions to you? If so, you might be in for a lengthy journey.

Later today I hope to watch the prayer service during which President Bush and Rev. Billy Graham will speak. I've invited Janice to come watch it with me. Perhaps both of us will gain strength.

I need your love and counsel more than ever.

Christ's peace to you,
Barbara

2

Tuesday, September 18, 2001
(Six days after being shut down, the stock market responded on this day, symbolizing America's determination to defeat terrorism).
Charleston, South Carolina

Dear Barbara,

I have read your September 14 letter over and over again. I wish that I could be with you now. Hopefully, before long I can travel to New York City.

I have thought of little else but you, Janice, Michelle, Tony, and the many others whose lives and families have been so monstrously disrupted by these senseless acts of terror.

The contrast between Charleston and New York City today is striking. While rescue crews struggle to find survivors in the debris of the Trade Center, Charleston has never been more beautiful. Though fall is coming, the city is still resplendent in crepe-myrtle, magnolias, and chrysanthemums. The pecan trees are loaded this year. The harvest will be abundant. Yesterday I took my boat up the Ashley River just to see the colorful flower gardens that grace lawns between the houses and the marsh. In a few weeks the temperatures here will still be in the mid-60s, and the New York City rescue workers could be battling cold weather. The beauty of Charleston, and September upon the harbor, have been partially eclipsed by the catastrophe in New York City.

Now, about Janice's determination to "have it out with God." No, I am not alarmed by your language, and I doubt that God is either. I suspect that on occasion some of God's defenders actually succeed in revealing their own insecurities rather than doing Him a service.

If the Book of Habakkuk is any indicator, Janice will not be the first one to hurl hard questions in God's direction. In the closing years of the seventh century B.C., the Babylonians were advancing on Jerusalem, killing, pillaging, and raping as they went. About that time the prophet Habakkuk put the following paraphrased question to God: "Are You God, or are You not?" Apparently thinking that his language was insufficiently direct, Habakkuk had another go at it: "Maybe You are a coward. Maybe You do well as God only when the big boys are not around. But when the Babylonians show up, You cower along with the rest of us!" In one last charge, Habakkuk demanded of God, "Either put up or shut up!" (1:2-17). Now, what do you think of a God who would allow a trusted friend to speak that way—and live to tell about it?

I have always been astonished by the fact that Habakkuk's attack didn't seem to rattle God. He let the old prophet "have at Him" and then allowed the Book of Habakkuk to become a part of the Bible. That episode in Israel's journey with God has caused me to suspect that He isn't as unnerved by honest questions as are many of His jittery protectors.

Maybe I am one of God's jittery protectors. Maybe I am searching frantically for ways to prop Him up, all the while telling Habakkuk to be quiet! Time will tell, because I intend to stay with you and Janice throughout the conversation.

Barbara, when I was a young parish priest, I was deeply plagued by the reality and problem of evil. At one point I thought that my theological and intellectual struggles would drive me from the ministry. That did not happen. Through much prayer, timely counsel from an older priest, and reading, I arrived at some answers that have made it possible for me to declare the gospel with faithfulness and integrity.

However, you should know that I have never arrived at solutions that can neutralize the hard questions raised by the reality of evil.

Often the problem of evil, my faith in God, and I—the three of us—engage in fierce debates. Frankly, I don't anticipate things being otherwise anytime soon. I value a statement by Frank Littell: "In the face of the deepest mystery of life and death, thoughtless utterance and premature closure are but the babbling of fools."

Barbara, I am praying for our nation and our world. I am also praying for you, Janice, and the children. I pray that Larry will be found alive, but I recognize that hope is dwindling. Janice must be aware of this as well. I am heavily invested in Janice's growth as a Christian. At the end of this dark night of the soul, I am confident that there is an enduring peace for her. But getting there will not be easy.

Barbara, don't be misled into thinking that faith comes easily for me. I pray regularly: "Lord, I believe; help thou mine unbelief" (Mark 9:24, KJV). This morning I prayed the following prayer for you, Janice, Larry, the children, myself, and for our grieving nation:

"O merciful Father, who hast taught us in thy holy Word that thou dost not willingly afflict or grieve the children of men: Look with pity upon the sorrows of [us] thy servant[s] for whom our prayers are offered. Remember [us], O Lord, in mercy, nourish [our] soul[s] with patience, comfort [us] with a sense of thy goodness, lift up thy countenance upon [us], and give [us] peace; through Jesus Christ our Lord. Amen" ("For a Person in Trouble or Bereavement," in "Prayers," in *The Book of Common Prayer*, 1979, No. 55).

When there is news regarding Larry, please call me immediately. I will await the questions you and Janice want to raise.

His grace to you,
Uncle Carl

[**A note to the reader:** Early on the morning of Wednesday, September 21, 2001, rescue workers located Larry's left arm. They were able to identify him by the description Janice had given of his wedding ring and initials on it.

[Janice said that never had she known such engulfing loneliness. First her mother had died, then her father, and now Larry—all of them gone. Her grief was compounded by the mounting death toll being reported by Mayor Rudolph Giuliani.

[Barbara called her uncle. He flew from Charleston to New York City to be with Janice in her time of grief. He arrived on Thursday evening, September 22, and remained until Sunday, September 25, when he returned to Charleston. Firefighters from many companies were present for the memorial service for Larry. Many people from the community attended. Never had Janice experienced such expressions of concern. The city showed that it cared.

[During Carl's stay in New York City, he and Barbara spoke only briefly and not substantially about the topic she had asked her uncle to discuss. Clearly, Carl's visit was a godsend for Janice and Barbara. Janice's grief was just beginning, but through Carl's counsel and prayers, she took some baby steps toward healing.]

3

Monday, October 1, 2001
New York City

Dear Uncle Carl,

I have been grading student essays all morning and am more than ready to take a break. If anyone doubts either the importance or the difficulty of teaching students how to comprehend and appreciate literature, let him or her work as a teacher of literature in a college or university for one year! A believer will emerge.

Words are inadequate for expressing the importance of your support for Janice during the most dreadful days of her life. Wherever you go, Uncle Carl, you seem to spread a sense of peace and hope. Your quiet faith, as you say, "in the God who raised His Son from the dead," is contagious. Janice and I have borrowed freely from your strength.

We in New York City are astonished by the outpouring of love and support for us. People have posted to the Internet hundreds of photos from cities around the world showing the displays of solidarity and grief during our period of grief. School children from Alabama sent more than 10,000 letters of encouragement to the rescue workers at "ground zero." In a beautiful turnabout, residents of Oklahoma City, all too familiar with collective sorrow, sent hundreds of teddy bears to the Red Cross to distribute to the families of the victims.

How will Janice ever be able to live without Eddie and Larry? The joy they brought her was a major source of strength and her motivation. When she dared to dream, it was usually because of Larry.

While "rescue" workers at "ground zero" continue to dig through the rubble hunting for signs of life, most people realize that hopes are fading that more survivors will be pulled from the wreckage. You have probably seen the pictures of family members of victims who brought pictures of their missing relatives to the scene. Perhaps you also saw the picture of the firefighters raising the flag in the midst of the rubble. When bodies are removed from the debris the workers and a chaplain gather for a very brief moment of prayer before returning to what has become simply a cleanup of the wreckage. It seems impossible to gauge the impact of death and destruction on the hundreds of heroic rescue workers.

The death toll in New York City has not been determined. Almost 5,000 people are still missing. Mayor Giuliani has stated that rescue workers will probably not be able to recover everyone. The casualties include Rev. Mychal Judge, a fire department chaplain. The 68-year-old friar had rushed from his 12- by 15-foot room at St. Francis of Assisi Friary to "ground zero" to offer comfort. He was administering last rites when he was killed by falling rubble. The "formal" toll from the airplane passengers in the Pennsylvania crash, the Trade Center, and the Pentagon totals 579.

Thanksgiving and Christmas are coming soon. Janice's mother is dead, and now her husband and father are also dead. The holidays will be very difficult ones for Janice and many people like her. Wesley and Sandy Thomas, who have three lively girls, have invited Janice and the kids and me to share Thanksgiving dinner with them.

Uncle Carl, I shared with Janice the prayer you placed at the end of your letter. The hope and faith it expressed gripped both of us. We were also impacted by the words Rev. Billy Graham spoke during the September 14 prayer service.

Janice continues to bombard me with questions I can't answer. Over coffee yesterday, she asked, "Why worship and love a God who either could have but did not—or wanted to but could not—prevent the September 11 holocaust?" She added, "Barbara, would you have tried to keep the attacks from occurring if you could have?"

"Of course," I answered.

"Do you believe that a perfectly good God would always try to eliminate evil so far as He could?" she countered.

I thought for a moment and then said, "Why, of course!"

She wasn't through: "Are there limits to what an omnipotent God could do?"

I was already over my head. But I tried. "None that I can think of," I muttered.

Janice smiled glumly. Her grief is adding to the power of her questions.

While I was trying to come up with a sensible reply, Janice hit me with another question. "Must believers deceive themselves?" she said. "Must we abandon honesty before we can love and worship God?"

Uncle Carl, I think the time has come to deal with Janice's questions regarding God and evil. Based on my conversations with her, I know that there are some rules that must be obeyed. I hope that I can summarize them correctly. For one thing, it is clear that the only God Janice wants to discuss is the God of the Bible, who is affirmed to be both all-powerful and all-loving. Trying to dance around either of these foundational assumptions will alienate her. She has no interest in nifty footwork. Similarly, defending some lesser deity, or creating a defensible god crafted by a philosopher, will not satisfy Janice. Either the God of the Bible or nothing at all.

Another important point for Janice is honesty. She will have nothing to do with answers for the problem of evil that come at the expense of honesty. She will reject all counsel that claims to have dealt faithfully with evil when in fact it has not. No tricks of logic that "take God off the hook."

Also, Janice will demand that evil be treated with the seriousness it deserves. She is repulsed, and so am I, by those who save God by dismissing the seriousness of evil and suffering. Janice is dismayed when Christians minimize the problem by converting evil into something good. I have heard people say that, in time, we will see that God meant everything for our good. Or I have heard others say that in time we will see the good in everything that happens. I once heard a minister tell grieving parents that the reason their child had been killed by a drunk driver was because God needed "another flower in heaven." I don't buy that.

Uncle Carl, making evil less than evil is not a good way to resolve the problem. When a five-year-old child is raped by someone who was supposed to be her protector, that cruelty will never become good. I believe that trying to make it so brutalizes the child a second time. When thousands of people are blasted into eternity by religious and political fanatics, that is evil. No degree of "community goodwill" can transform it into anything else.

Why can't some of God's "defenders" understand this? Some of their "solutions" actually drive people away from Him. I don't deny that many times something good emerges out of what seemed to be hopeless despair. But that doesn't for one moment change the fact that evil is evil. It is destructive, abusive, and alienating. It can't be changed into anything else. Honest and sensitive persons won't try.

By now you probably can't tell whether I am speaking for Janice or for myself. I'm not sure either.

You know, Uncle Carl, except for Aunt Louise, whom I have never really known, and a few distant cousins, you are my family. Yours has been an enduring love. Maybe you have forgotten, but do you remember when I was a little girl and I ate fresh Lowcountry figs in the backseat of your Pontiac? I can still recall the sticky little handprints on the rear windows and upholstery. Mostly, though, I remember you patiently washing my hands, the doors, and the windows. Was the backseat ever usable again?

Please write soon.

His peace,
Barbara

4

Friday, October 5, 2001
Charleston, South Carolina

Dear Barbara,

I have carefully read your highly informative and provocative letter. Last Sunday I was the guest celebrant and preacher in a Savannah church. In the afternoon, before my return to Charleston, I sat on the Riverfront Plaza, watching the parade of freighters and pug-nosed tugs pass by. Across the way stands the convention center and hotel that replaced the old wharfs. I thought of some of the famous people the Savannah River has brought to this point—Gen. James Oglethorpe, John Wesley, and Gen. William Tecumseh Sherman. While sitting there, I also pondered Janice's questions and began to formulate a response.

My time with you was too short. If, as you say, my being there for Larry's memorial service was helpful to Janice and you, the two of you were even more so to me. When I observe your indomitable spirit, I think of your mother. I recall that as a child nothing seemed to defeat her for very long. I remember once when I hid her dolls, she just chose other toys and changed the game. That dampened my enthusiasm for meanness.

Without intending to do so, Janice has actually stated the problem of evil in a somewhat novel way. According to the Bible, she is correct to think (as her statement implies) that God is both all-loving and all-powerful, or omnipotent. If either of these affirmations can be successfully denied, then what the Bible says about God is not true, and our faith is in vain. I know of no way to avoid this conclusion.

In her own way, Janice has said that either God wanted to prevent the September 11 destruction of lives and property but could not, or He could have prevented the carnage but did not want to.

For the sake of clarity, let's try one more statement. John Hick is a famous philosopher of religion. He has posed the problem of evil in a way that makes sense to me: if God is all-loving, then He must desire to abolish moral evil. If He is all-powerful, He must be able to abolish evil. But evil exists in abundance. Often it appears to be unrestrained. Therefore, God cannot be both all-loving and all-powerful. He could be one or the other but not both. In either case He is not God.

Unless we are willing to attribute some good purpose to a God who would choose to allow such destruction as occurred on September 11, we seem forced to choose between His being either all-loving but not all-powerful, or all-powerful but not all-loving. In either instance, He is not the God of the Bible.

To say that an all-loving God chose to stand aside while hundreds of people died at the hands of terrorists, and that He did so to accomplish some good purpose, is morally and religiously absurd. If mortal rescue workers put their lives at risk to remove survivors, then surely an omnipotent and all-loving God would go a step further. He would desire to protect the vulnerable and to safeguard the innocent. If we have to deny this, then the God of the Bible will evaporate.

On the other hand, even if by some wild stretch of the imagination we were to think that God allowed the killings in order to accomplish some good purpose, all people of wisdom would remain silent. They would recognize the impossibility of speaking intelligently about the nature, purposes, and actions of such a God. The most responsible "talk" about God would be no talk at all.

One of my professors in seminary, Nels F. S. Ferré, said at the end of World War II, "As Christians, evil is always our central problem. Today we are almost overwhelmed by it." At the time, I didn't catch the importance of his statement. After years of ministry, I now understand it more clearly.

I have told you of how the prophet Habakkuk helps me. Another prophet wrestled with the problem of evil—Jeremiah, the one who didn't want to be a prophet in the first place.

When arguing with God, Jeremiah figured he was up against unfair odds, but he raised his questions anyway: "O Lord, I will dispute with thee, for thou art just; yes, I will plead my case before thee. Why do the wicked prosper and traitors live at ease?" (12:1, NEB). Jeremiah thought the consequences of evil were unjustly distributed—and the apparent prosperity of the wicked made no sense to him. Jeremiah would have found a friend in Robert McAffee Brown, who admitted, "The mystery of evil is the source of our greatest vulnerability as believers."

Barbara, with regard to Janice's three rules for discussion, I concur wholeheartedly. We will (1) discuss the God of the Bible, all-loving and all-powerful, (2) be honest and faithful as we deal with the problem of evil, and (3) treat the problem of evil with the seriousness it deserves. Maybe Janice will benefit from a discovery I made early in my ministry.

Once I was trying to minister to a father whose wife and two children had been killed by a drunk driver. Most of my efforts to exonerate God wound up either making Him smaller or trivializing the evil. I was having a very difficult time of it. I found myself shouting inwardly, "Why doesn't God speak for himself?" As I worked through that crisis over subsequent months, it dawned on me that the more profound and rich our understanding of God, the more acute the problem of evil. I have thought for a long time that many people—laypeople, clergy, and scholars—succeed in diminishing evil by diminishing God. Some solution!

By the way, some of the fig stains were still on the backseat when I sold the car. "Uncle Carl, did I do dat?" you asked over and over. You were only four years old.

I will anticipate your next letter.

With love and prayers,
Uncle Carl

5

Sunday, October 14, 2001
New York City

Dear Uncle Carl,

Your letter made me envious. Sitting on the Riverfront Plaza in Savannah would be a delight. I have not seen the new convention center and hotel. I remember well the time you and I spent almost one full day browsing in the shops along Factor's Walk. You took me to a famous boardinghouse for lunch. I can't remember the name, but I do remember the oysters and shrimp. It was a place where we had to bus our own dishes!

If things develop here as I hope, perhaps before the fall is over I can fly to Charleston for a visit. Maybe Janice and the kids can come along as well if you don't mind. Charleston would present a relief.

Thursday marked the one-month anniversary of the attack. So

much has happened since then. Janice has returned to work, but grief is etched on her face, and her voice is ragged with pain. She is making a little progress in accepting the reality of Larry's and Eddie's deaths. But no one can accept the absurdity of thousands of lives eliminated by moral cripples who knew how to crash airplanes into buildings!

As you would expect, in this area one regularly meets someone who lost a relative or a close friend in the collapse of the towers. The monstrous nature of the tragedy still hangs like a cloud over New York City. You would be pleased to see the many U.S. flags displayed all over the area. South of Newark a huge flag flies atop an extended crane.

Janice and I were gratified by the honesty of your October 15 letter. After reading your letter, Janice said, "Well, Uncle Carl is certainly not a coward." She was pleased to learn how closely her question paralleled John Hick's statement. Neither of us could remember having read Jeremiah's complaint. Janice was surprised to learn that a prophet could speak to God so frankly. "Maybe my questions won't damn me after all," she said through tears. I believe that Janice has found a friend in Jeremiah. The prophet reminds me that the writers of the Bible aren't so far removed from us as we sometimes imagine.

After reading your letter, Janice wanted me to explain what it means to say that God is both all-loving and all-powerful. After I had tried my best to respond, Janice said, "I think we had better ask Uncle Carl!" Actually, I thought that I had given a fairly good answer.

So, at Janice's request (and mine), please explain to us what it means to say that God is all-loving and all-powerful. We think we agree that if either of these is not true of God, then God as the Bible describes Him does not exist.

I have begun to sketch a novel that has the events of September 11 as its setting. Maybe one way to combat the insanity of terrorism is to paint a verbal portrait of the human and social toll that indiscriminate destruction takes on both perpetrators and victims. I want to tell the story from the perspective of the children who suffer.

Janice sends her appreciation and greetings to you.

In Christ's strength,
Barbara

6

Tuesday, October 23, 2001
Charleston, South Carolina

Dear Barbara,

The calendar says October, but the South Carolina sun tells me that summer has not passed! This weather helps explain why people flock to the "sunny South" during the winter. Charleston marina is still full of watercraft. Last night I walked the Battery and enjoyed the rippling breeze coming across the harbor. I know I sound like a provincial, but surely no scene surpasses the Charleston harbor at night. Its panorama of lights from bridges, ships, automobiles, forts, and houses sweeps from James Island to Mount Pleasant.

The Savannah restaurant to which you referred is Mrs. Wilkes's Boarding House. And you are correct—we bused our own dishes. Everyone does. If you and Janice come later this fall, we will go there. And I would be thrilled to have children around the house again, to hear their laughter echo off these walls.

I agree with you that in my efforts to deal with Janice's questions regarding the problem of evil, I need to explain "all-loving" and "all-powerful." Even though it seems that the reality of evil eliminates at least one of these, the Christian answer finally resides in both.

Barbara, unless both of these statements about God are preserved, evil ceases to be a religious problem. If He is not all-powerful, then the presence of evil in the world should probably surprise no one. The same would be true if He is not all-loving. Evil is a religious problem because the Bible makes both claims about God. A contemporary theologian has put the issue this way: "The sting in the question 'Why is there evil?' is God. The sting in the question 'Is there a God?' is evil."

There are famous thinkers who deal with the problem of evil by abandoning either God's omnipotence or His all-loving nature. They then proceed to solve the problem of evil, which astonishes me. They seem not to realize that after they have eliminated one of the essential qualities of God, there is no longer a problem to solve. Barbara, whole books are written by people who do this.

I will not make such an error. I hope that the carefulness with which I answer Janice's questions will not become tedious for either of you. I will not overwhelm you with theological jargon; but for our discussion to be helpful, I will have to lay a good foundation. Much mischief occurs when the phrases "all-powerful" and "all-loving" are improperly handled.

Let's begin with the phrase "all-powerful," which is another way of speaking of God's sovereignty and majesty. Some of the Bible's clearest statements regarding God as all-powerful occur in the second part of the Book of Isaiah. The prophet spoke of the sovereignty of God at a time when some would probably have advised Isaiah to keep his mouth shut. At the time, God certainly didn't seem to be all-powerful. Israel, the Northern Kingdom, had been destroyed by the Assyrians. Judah, the Southern Kingdom, had been destroyed by the Babylonians. Jerusalem and the Temple lay in ruins.

The prophet's words found in the second part of Isaiah were spoken while the Babylonian Empire was dissolving and its place of prominence was being taken by the Persians. News accounts of the day would not have mentioned the obscure God of the exiled Jews. He would not have been invited to a summit meeting for world leaders.

However, Isaiah didn't get his instructions by first reading the Babylonian Times or the Persian Sun. With clearer vision than world powers could provide, Isaiah had seen Yahweh, the real Shaper of world events. Of Him and for Him the prophet spoke. Chapters 40—43 help me understand God's sovereignty. In them an all-powerful, self-originating God, not limited at all by other pretenders, speaks decisively.

According to what God says of himself through Isaiah, He freely executes His purposes in the world, and no one or no nation can successfully obstruct them (43:3-9). By God's will and power alone, He "created the heavens and stretched them out, [he] spread out the earth and what comes from it, [he] gives breath to the people upon it and spirit to those who walk in it" (42:5, NRSV).

Four verses in particular provide a focus for chapters 40—43. First, "I am the LORD, that is my name; my glory I give to no other, nor my praise to idols" (42:8, NRSV). Second and third, "Before me no god was formed, nor shall there be any after me. I, I am the LORD, and besides me there is no savior" (43:10-11, NRSV). Fourth, "I am God, and also henceforth I am He; there is no one who can deliver from my hand; I work and who can hinder it?" (v. 13, NRSV). These verses offer a God who is free and totally unencumbered by efforts to frustrate His purposes. The chapters confirm that He is unfailingly faithful to himself and to His people, even when external circumstances indicate otherwise.

Nowhere in the Bible does God retract or modify what Isaiah records. What He says about himself through Isaiah parallels His answer when Moses asked how he should respond to the enslaved Israelites when they asked for God's name. He told Moses to tell them, "I AM WHO I AM" (Exod. 3:14, NRSV), or "I WILL BE WHAT I WILL BE" (RSV, margin), has sent you (see vv. 13-15). Spelled out, this means, "Tell the people that the One who alone can truly say, 'I am God, and there is no other,' has sent you." This means that God is the sole source of His own being. Everything else that exists—including the pharaoh—depends on God for its existence. He is God alone; He alone is God.

Both in the beginning and currently, the power for creatures to exist comes ultimately from God alone. All creativity demonstrated within the world is finally His gift. This truth has sometimes been put another way. Of God alone can it be said, "He is." Of everything else we must say that "it exists." God is the Source of His own being and the Source of the world's existence as well.

This concept is necessary for a proper understanding of God as Creator. To be sure, in varying degrees, the creation itself exhibits creativity and finite freedom. When God created humankind, He created us with real finite freedom. But ultimately our creativity and freedom are grounded in God, who both originates and sustains the world. By Him, the Book of Colossians says, "all things were created," and through Him all things are sustained (1:15-20). There are no independent sources of existence that can stand opposed to God.

Barbara, you can see from all of this that God is perfectly free to be himself; no external limitations or restraints can be forced upon Him. By contrast, of no creature can this be said. To exist as a creature is to be necessarily limited—by resources, time, location, intelligence, mortality, and so on. If God were so limited, He would not be God.

As surprising as it might seem, some people try to resolve the problem of evil by making God to some extent finite. They say that whether God likes it or not, the world imposes limitations on Him. In this world, they say, God is a fellow struggler. Take courage, they say. This seems to be Rabbi Harold Kushner's solution in *When Bad Things Happen to Good People.* You will recall that the book was a best-seller. Maybe making God finite is a solution for some, but the Bible calls such gods "idols." They must never be favorably compared with Yahweh.

Rabbi Kushner's book illustrates efforts to resolve the problem of evil by diminishing God. As it turns out, the cure is much worse than the disease. Frankly, I have no interest in a finite deity who is just one more fellow struggler, even if he is more powerful than we are. Such a god could never be the object of worship as the Bible describes worship.

Barbara, I hope I am not making you weary!

We need to take the discussion a step farther. To say that God is all-powerful also means that He is holy, "the Holy One." The word "holy" is synonymous with God. To put it another way, God is "wholly other" than what is finite and creaturely. Gustaf Aulén, a Swedish theologian who had quite an influence on me years ago, said that God's holiness establishes without question a definite line of demarcation between the divine and the merely human.

God is not limited (unless He chooses otherwise) by anything beyond himself. Yet, as Creator He sets the primary limits and conditions for everything else. In His presence there is only one appropriate creaturely attitude: worship.

I said that no external limitations can be imposed upon God by any creature. But perhaps God can place constraints upon himself. A self-imposed limitation would be quite in keeping with God being all-powerful. Let's use as an example a roughhousing father who allows his five-year-old "Power Puff Girl" daughter to "handcuff and put him in jail for the rest of his life." The sentence will probably last until the "Power Puff Girl" changes and orders her father to "become her horse." Obviously, the father has imposed limitations on himself because he wants to promote growth in his daughter. In doing so, the father demonstrates strength and love, not weakness.

The father's curtailment of his power is the logic of a love that desires the genuine freedom and growth of the child. The father could have forced the child to do all that he wanted her to do. But total control was not in accordance with his nature and will. Nor could total control have developed the potential in the child, the object of his love. Strength that can accept self imposed limitations is greater than strength that cannot.

Similarly, for purposes of creativity and covenant, the free God has chosen to make himself vulnerable. The father in my illustration could have "broken out of jail" anytime he wanted to but not without sacrificing growth in the child. As strange as it may seem, through God's self-imposed vulnerability He demonstrates His sovereignty, holiness, and love.

God could choose to eliminate His vulnerability and establish a world where there is absolute predictable order. But think of all that would be sacrificed in the process. For starters, put personhood at the top of the list.

In the presence of a God who is vulnerable in this way, a human history with finite freedom and real novelty can appear. If the Bible is read carefully, it becomes clear that in creating humankind, God intended to form a free covenant partner who could receive and return love. God did not set out to create mechanical robots but real people with finite freedom. The Bible leads us to believe that when love characterizes the relationship between God and humankind, both are enriched. The vulnerability of God also means that He suffers if His covenant partner breaks the terms of the covenant. The prophets said that God takes humankind so seriously that He is injured by human disobedience.

God's history with us his creatures reveals His self-imposed vulnerability. God has opened His heart in His covenant with us.

A marvelous paradox is displayed as the Bible describes the all-powerful and vulnerable God. Some of the best-known examples are the Suffering Servant of Isaiah 53 and the Book of Hosea.

Ultimately, the paradox is manifest in the person and work of Jesus Christ. According to the Christian faith, the supreme expression of God's self-imposed vulnerability is His suffering love expressed on the Cross. "But God, who is rich in mercy, out of the great love with which he loved us, even when we were dead through our trespasses, made us alive together with Christ (by grace you have been saved), and raised us up with him" (Eph. 2:4-6). No greater declaration of God's suffering love exists than John 3:16: "For God so loved the world, that he gave . . ." (KJV).

Don't conclude too quickly that God's self-imposed limits resolve the problem of evil. As we shall see later on, in some ways His self-imposed vulnerability actually makes the problem more difficult.

Barbara, it is nearing late afternoon here, and my flower garden is crying for attention. When I look at my water bill next month, I will need to believe that I didn't spend the money watering weeds. I will try to pick up the discussion tomorrow.

Thursday, October 25, 2001

A confession is in order from me. Yesterday my neighbor convinced me to go with him to Lake Moultrie to fish. Then he insisted that we stop in Summerville at the Barbecue Barn for supper. Well, here I am, finally back on station.

We were ready to deal with the question "What does it mean to say that God is all-loving?" For starters, just as God is holy, God is love (1 John 4:8, 16). Love isn't just something God does—it's who He *is*. Love is the expression of God's being, and His holiness establishes the character of His love. Together, love and holiness constitute God's essence, His innermost character.

The Epistle of 1 John teaches that God is the Fountainhead of all love (4:7). Without any ambiguity, He is a God of love and mercy. Swedish theologian Gustaf Aulén said, "Nothing can be said about God, his power, his opposition to evil, or anything else, which is not in the last analysis a statement about his love." This puts the focus where it ought to be.

As the active expression of God's being, His love always acts to manifest His glory and majesty, to make Him known. The relationship between His love and His power is absolutely essential, even though this makes the problem of evil immensely more acute.

Now, let's add another element to our discussion. God always employs His power for the purpose of achieving love's designs. Anyone who tries to deny this should be ready to watch Him unravel. The power of God is the power of His love. If God is love, and if love is not just something He sometimes does, then in exercising His power, He exercises His love.

Now, take another step. According to the New Testament, in the person and work of Christ, God's definitive self-disclosure occurred. When we look at Christ, we behold in Him, without ambiguity, the God who is holy love. In Him, God was incarnate. Through Him, God sought out sinful humankind and established communion with us.

Let's talk more about the positive content of God's love. First, His love is spontaneous or unconditional. Second, His love is self-giving, even when there is no promise that love will be reciprocated (John 3:16). Third, the love of God is unfailingly creative and redemptive. In both creation and redemption, His love brings into existence what would not have existed otherwise. The stories of the lost sheep and the lost son beautifully illustrate this (Luke 15:3-7, 11-24). A major dimension of love's creativity is that God acts to establish justice in all the earth. Fourth, His love is sovereign; it cannot be silenced, immobilized, or finally frustrated by evil. Nothing in all the Bible is more amazing than this. Love finds a way (Rom. 5:8; 8:28-39). Permit me to use Gustaf Aulén again: "God's sovereignty is entirely a sovereignty of love. There is no divine power which is not the power of love."

"Hold on a moment," you might ask. "Aren't sovereignty and love mutually exclusive? Doesn't sovereignty mean unqualified dominance?" Barbara, herein lies a central Christian paradox, a redemptive one.

So far as I am concerned, we have arrived at the center of the Christian faith. In the cross of our Lord, God made a definitive statement regarding himself. *"Vulnerable love* will win when *invulnerable coercion* has fallen exhausted,"* He essentially said at Calvary. "Only vulnerable, suffering love can achieve what I have in mind for My creation."

As I said earlier, an invulnerable God who eliminates all risks to himself could certainly have it His way. But an invulnerable God cannot achieve lively covenant with His creation. He cannot develop freed sons and daughters who willingly enjoy relationship with Him and who mature into adulthood to reflect His image.

Am I making this clear? The vulnerability of God's love doesn't mean that His sovereignty is eliminated or even diminished. It simply clarifies the meaning of divine sovereignty and distinguishes it from raw power. God does not coerce us to love or obey Him. But we must be careful not to confuse vulnerability with permissiveness. The God of vulnerable love has purposes for history and designs for His creation. He acts patiently and decisively to achieve them all.

Barbara, be patient with me a little longer. There is one more dimension of God's love we must examine. We dare not miss it, even though it makes the problem of evil even more difficult. God always opposes what is opposed to love. This is simply another way of saying that He opposes what is opposed to himself. It is also one way to talk about His righteousness.

When we say that God acts righteously, we mean that He is acting in a manner faithful to himself as Holy Love. He is declaring His Majesty. His righteousness includes His defending the moral structures He intends for us. Negatively stated, God's righteousness is His comprehensive opposition to evil, to all that opposes love.

God does not and could not make alliances with evil. The Book of Sirach in the Apocrypha says that God "has no need of the sinful [person]. The Lord hates all abominations; such things are not loved by those who fear him" (Sirach 15:12-13, NRSV). Although the statement is not biblical, it agrees with the Bible.

Among those who err in trying to resolve the problem of evil, there is as much error here as at any point. Many of God's would-be defenders find strange ways to make evil necessary for achieving His purposes. I have often heard people say that we cannot mature as persons unless we experience sorrow. Or people say that we can't know the value of goodness unless we experience evil. If either of these statements is true, then God is inescapably bound to an alliance with evil. Nonsense! This does not exclude the fact that we may grow as a result of how we respond to evil. But this is a far cry from saying that God somehow "needs" evil to accomplish His will.

By now you have probably decided that if the terms "all-powerful" and "all-loving" mean what I have said, then God has a very serious problem on His hands. When these affirmations about Him are properly understood, the problem of evil becomes more, rather than less, intense. If God's power and love are inseparably united, if He really does oppose all that opposes love, then the September 11 attacks "just shouldn't have happened."

The prospects of your visit later in the fall have buoyed my spirits enormously. I immediately began thinking of special places in the Lowcountry I would like to show Janice.

Barbara, today I have prayed a collect for guidance found in *The Book of Common Prayer.* I want to share it with you: "O heavenly Father, in whom we live and move and have our being: We humbly pray thee so to guide and govern us by thy Holy Spirit, that in all the cares and occupations of our life we may not forget thee, but remember that we are ever walking in thy sight; through Jesus Christ our Lord. Amen."

I will greatly anticipate your response.

Love,
Uncle Carl

7

Wednesday, October 31, 2001
New York City

Dear Uncle Carl,

I forgive you for going fishing when you were supposed to be writing to me.

As I'm sure you have seen on the news, the final ragged remnant of the Trade Center is all that is left standing. Under the debris of the towers is a couple billion dollars in gold reserves that belong to nations around the world. While viewing the television coverage of the wreckage and a report on the millions of tons of rubble covering the gold reserves, I was again overcome by a sense of disbelief. How could so much suffering and destruction be unleashed so quickly on so many families?

Uncle Carl, Janice and I, with a Bible before us, have studied your letter almost phrase by phrase. You really put us through the paces! As we read, both of us experienced a strange mixture of responses. On the one hand, we found ourselves drawn to worship the God you described. On the other hand, as the letter progressed, Janice asked, half seriously, "Is Uncle Carl trying to extol God, or setting Him up for a terrible fall?" I am beginning to understand why you said that the richer one's vision of God, the more difficult the problem of evil. In our opinion, you have increased the intensity of the problem. Are you sure you want to do this?

I will say this much about what you have written—you would rather face a topic honestly and be bloodied in the process than to escape as an unscathed coward.

A friend of Janice gave to her a statement by a Jewish theologian named Richard Rubenstein. Rubenstein says that "a God who tolerates the sufferings of even one innocent child is either infinitely cruel or hopelessly indifferent." Perhaps largely because of the thousands of children who lost a parent in the September 11 attacks, Rubenstein's statement has impacted Janice rather deeply.

A few days ago I remembered that in Joseph Heller's novel *Catch-22*, the character Yossarian levels a strong accusation against God. I showed it to Janice. She said that Yossarian had expressed some of her deepest sentiments. She suggested that I share the quote with you. See if you agree that Yossarian's accusation sounds a little bit like a modern-day Habakkuk:

> And don't tell me God works in mysterious ways; there's nothing so mysterious about it. He's not working at all. He's playing. Or else he's forgotten all about us. That's the kind of God you people talk about—a country bumpkin, a clumsy, bungling, brainless, conceited, uncouth hayseed . . . how much reverence can you have for a supreme being who finds it necessary to include such phenomena as phlegm and tooth decay in his divine system of creation? What in the world was running through that warped, evil, scatological mind of his when he robbed old people of the power to control their bowel movements. . . . What a colossal, immortal blunderer! When you consider the opportunity and power he had . . . and then look at the stupid, ugly little mess he made of it instead, his sheer incompetence is almost staggering. It's obvious he never met a payroll. Why, no self-respecting businessman would hire a bungler like him as even a shipping clerk.

Uncle Carl, although Yossarian's language may be rather shocking to some, he has honestly voiced the thoughts of many people. Truthfully, I find his honesty more attractive than the superficial explanations of evil that some of God's defenders offer.

Last Sunday after church, Janice and I fell into conversation with Jeff, who is a philosophy professor at an area college. He is a member of my Bible study group. As we told him about our exchange of letters with you, his eyes sparkled. The problem of evil is one of his topics of special interest.

Jeff gave to us Augustine's version of the problem of evil. It goes something like this: "Either God cannot abolish evil, or He will not. If He wants to do so but cannot, then He is not all powerful. On the other hand, if He could eliminate evil but chooses not to, He is not all-loving. In either case the God of the Bible vanishes." Jeff offered to assist by providing resources that will help Janice and me formulate our questions. We gladly accepted his offer. So, if you hear us raising questions that go beyond our expertise, give Jeff the credit.

Jeff told us that from a Christian perspective, before one can get to the more serious attempts to resolve the problem of evil, there are a number of more superficial "solutions" that have to be cleared away. He started to identify them and used language that quickly left us shaking our heads. He noticed our eyes glazing over and then said, "Your uncle will know what I'm talking about." Is that true? If so, I hope that you will translate your explanations into lay language!

On Monday [October 29] I joined the crowds of relatives and friends of victims and made my way to ground zero where the Trade Centers had stood. Thousands of us listened to the memorial service while staring in disbelief at the devastation. "Hellish," one newspaper wrote of the devastation. The words describe more than the building. I still find it incomprehensible that so much destruction and suffering could have been caused by a few crazed terrorists.

The thousands of people standing before the twisted wreckage represented an expanding ring of grief. I was dumbstruck by the pain and disbelief that radiated from their faces. We were standing before what was still a temporary tomb for hundreds of people.

Janice and I still hope that we can come to Charleston, perhaps in early January. But I am not so confident as I was earlier. Virginia, my department chairperson, has asked if I might be willing to represent her during a January conference in Dallas. Virginia's husband has been ill for months. Unless his condition improves, Virginia will have to skip the conference to care for him. If I go to Dallas, Janice and I will probably have to postpone our Charleston trip until the university's spring break. But I hope that won't be necessary.

Love to the most patient uncle in the world.

Grace and peace,
Barbara

8

Thursday, November 8, 2001
Charleston, South Carolina

Dear Barbara,

I received your letter on Saturday. I read it once and then on Sunday took it with me to Beaufort, where I was to be the guest celebrant in the St. Helena Parish Church. Upon stepping into the St. Helena Church, one is transported back to the late 1700s. The church is surrounded by a cemetery, which is in turn surrounded by an ancient brick wall. The church building has been magnificently preserved. You may recall that the Beaufort area was the setting for *The Sea Island Lady*. The town and its elegant antebellum mansions, so exquisitely preserved, have been the setting for numerous movies.

Before I made the 60-mile trip back up the coast to Charleston, I drove a few extra miles to the Old Sheldon Church. Before the American Revolution the church building was a magnificent structure, one of the grandest in colonial South Carolina. Now the church is only a shell. The front columns, walls, and most of the arches over the windows still stand as haunting reminders of the building's former beauty. The structure was burned by the British, rebuilt, and then destroyed by the invading Union army. Old Sheldon Church is a grim reminder of how war is no respecter of either people or structures.

Some of the 18th- and 19th-century above-ground brick graves behind the church are still in place. I sat down by one of them to read your letter. But my mind was drawn to the many colonists who once came to worship in Old Sheldon Church. Ironically, while leaning against a grave, I thought of the violence of war that had long ago caught up those worshipers. Leaning against mortality and contemplating the results of violence! What a way to spend a Sunday afternoon!

So now there are three of you to deal with. First a computer consultant, then a professor of literature, and now a professor of philosophy! Who will you add next?

Well, Jeff is correct. Not all the efforts to resolve the problem of evil should be treated with equal seriousness. But because even the less important ones are often mentioned and seriously proposed, they must be considered.

Early this morning, as I was clearing weeds and grass from around some rose bushes, an idea came to me. Why not deal with the less serious approaches to the problem of evil as though I am weeding around flowers? I'll pull the small ones first and then later focus on the more important "solutions."

There is no special order to the "weeds," except that some are probably larger than others. First, many Christians believe that God meticulously governs every event in life. There is no real freedom in the creation. No part of the creation has any real distance from God. Everything that happens occurs because that's the way God wants it. Supporters of meticulous providence think that anything less compromises God's sovereignty. Under no conditions would they ever say that God is vulnerable, as I have done. Vulnerability and sovereignty are for them incompatible concepts.

I heard a story of a person who held to this position. One day he started down the stairs into the basement of his house. As he did, he tripped over a roller skate and tumbled all the way to the bottom of the stairs. Bruised all over, he sat up and said, "Well, thank God that much is over with!" At least he was consistent.

Barbara, I am told that the explanation of evil by "meticulous providence" gives great confidence to those who hold it. Respectfully, the position arises from a desire to defend God's sovereignty. But it has driven many persons into atheism. And understandably so.

Such a God can indeed be an all-powerful God. But by no definition known to reasonable people can such a God be called all-loving. In the presence of a brutally raped five-year-old child, only a moral pigmy could dare speak of such a God as "all-loving." One reason we call evil "evil" is that it is pointless and destructive. No amount of maneuvering can make it otherwise. Those who love as love is normally defined and experienced could never love a God who is the author of evil.

Second, some have said that calling God into question because of evil is wrong because He no longer has anything to do with the world. Even though He created the world, He is now just a silent spectator. When He created the world, He gave freedom to the creation. From then on there would be no further particular divinely initiated acts in the world. Therefore, He should not be blamed for particular evils.

Epicurus, the Greek philosopher, and Albert Camus, the French novelist, held positions similar to this. God is neither positively nor negatively involved in the world. So He can't be implicated in moral evil.

You will recognize this "solution" as similar to deism. You know more about the 18th-century deists than I. They thought that God, having once created the world, is no longer active in it.

Deism is still attractive for many as a way to explain how God can be reconciled with the reality of evil. But the solution won't work, not if we are discussing the God of the Bible. Although deism claims to take God off the hook, it doesn't. It is difficult to know the significance of a "passive God." Removing God from the crime scene may seem to release Him from involvement in evil, but it doesn't succeed. No court would allow God to create and then just walk away from a world like this.

At any rate, the deist God and the God of the Bible have almost nothing in common. Even though the Bible doesn't always make clear just how God works in the world, it doesn't allow for a passive God. The Bible gives many reasons for rejecting this solution, the most important of which is the incarnation of God in Christ. The God who loved the world so much that He was willing to give His only begotten Son to achieve its reconciliation is hardly a silent, indifferent spectator. Furthermore, the deist God could never be the Heavenly Father who raised Jesus from the dead. Also, according to Jesus, God "clothes the grass of the field" and gives beauty to the lilies (Matt. 6:30; see vv. 25-33).

I need to qualify my critique of the deist solution. Most of us have found it attractive at one time or another. At times we've all asked, "God, where are You?" or "Where were You?" The implication of the questions is that God has been passive when He should have been active.

I know that one of your favorite writers is Franz Kafka. In his novel *The Castle,* you probably recall the frustration the main character, K., faced in his efforts to make contact with the Castle. K. was a land surveyor who had abandoned home and family to work for the count of the Castle. But no matter how long he waited in the village below, K. never succeeded in his effort to gain clear instructions from the count. Though his frustrations were endless, K. never relaxed his struggle and would die worn-out by his efforts.

Kafka, you will recall, thought that a similar frustration awaits those who try to understand God's relationship with the world. They will live and die frustrated by the effort. God and ultimate meaning are simply not available to us. Why not humbly accept this fact and give up the quest?

According to our newspaper, during the September 14 prayer service in Washington, D.C., Billy Graham said he has been asked literally hundreds of times, "Why does God allow tragedy?" He said his answer is "I don't know." His honesty was refreshing. But Kafka would have asked, "Then why, Rev. Graham, since evil is such an incomprehensible mystery, do you insist on speaking with such confidence about God? In the interest of honesty and intelligence, shouldn't you just shut up?"

Although I don't agree with Kafka's conclusions, I certainly do respect the experiences of many that have led them to the frustration his character K. experienced. The faith of many has been shaken because it seems that the God in whom they have placed their trust acts in ways that are unintelligible or contradictory.

One more note regarding God as the silent spectator—I have often heard it said that once He had created the world with its laws of gravity and consequences, He couldn't go around interrupting those laws willy-nilly. He couldn't interrupt the law of gravity just to keep a child from dropping once she had fallen from a window. If He were to do so, He would destroy the very order He had created. Put another way, one can't depend on gravity to hold one's car on the road and at the same time want gravity suspended to keep the car from crashing into a gully if the car leaves the roadway. In an orderly world, gravity assures both results.

I have heard Christians use this argument. But at the same time they are unwilling to give up the notion of miracles. They seem to believe that in rare and wonderful instances God sets aside the law of gravity, and so on, without doing any harm to orderliness in the world. When I have asked, "If God can do this even once without destroying order, why can't He always do it?" I have yet to hear a responsible answer.

A third weed is that evil is explainable because God is himself a madman who gives us both Bethlehem and the ovens of Auschwitz, both shepherds and S.S. guards. The psychologist Carl Jung, for example, thought that by advocating a bad God, he could solve the problem of evil. This "solution" emerges only when those who embrace it unhitch their thinking from the Bible. There we find no schizophrenic madman. Instead, we encounter a God of steadfast love.

One more little weed to be plucked is the claim that moral evil is simply the inevitable by-product of the struggle and waste involved in the evolutionary process. We won't have to wait long for a good reason to reject this argument. Any solution that makes moral evil inevitable immediately implicates God as evil. Later, we will meet this solution in a more sophisticated form. For now, let us say that if God were to originate something that was unavoidably flawed from the start, then He could not escape the dominant share of blame for evil. If that were the case, then He too would need a savior. As a matter of fact, He would be the principal candidate for forgiveness. He certainly could not be the Savior we meet in the Bible.

The idea that evil is inevitable is certainly not the message given in the Genesis creation accounts (chapters 1—3). According to those chapters, the world that God created was good. Adam and Eve were God's good creation. They were warned against committing evil. The clear indication is that the evil they did commit should not have happened. Provisions for not choosing evil were made available to them.

Nowhere in the Bible does this positive estimate of God's creation change. Forgiveness for evils committed is offered, but evil is never treated as inevitable. Always evil is an intruder in God's creation. It is antagonistic to His will and His designs for the creation.

Barbara, are you still with me? If so, let's tackle a few larger weeds. The first one is the claim that evil is not real. According to this solution, the problem of evil evaporates when we realize that evil is only an illusion. It is just a wrong way of viewing life. According to exponents of this idea, evil has no more power and reality than we are willing to give it.

Christian Scientists, for example, say that the reality of evil reaches no farther than the mind. All we need for dismissing the problem of evil is to think correctly about God and life. Buddhism offers a similar solution.

One can sometimes hear well-intended Christians saying something similar. They do so first by minimizing evil. "In time, you will see that what you thought to be evil was actually good," they might say. Now, most of us have been surprised to learn that an event we thought harmful and undesirable actually turned out to be beneficial. But we ought not generalize from this common experience to dismiss the reality of evil. You may recall that Father Paneloux, the Jesuit priest in *The Plague,* tells his congregation that God "unfailingly transforms evil into good." But a drive-by shooting in the city's urban core that snuffs out the life of a mother's child will never be good. Nor can the brutal rape of a six-year-old ever be explained away as an "illusion" or as "good in disguise." This is evil, and the Christian faith has no interest in calling it anything else.

Standard Christian doctrine teaches that evil does not exist as an independent reality. If God alone is the Creator, then there is no independent realm of being that we can call evil. Instead, evil is parasitic in nature. It lives by preying upon and distorting God's good creation. It is a distortion or perversion of what God created and called good. Like the gambling industry, it generates no wealth of its own. But even so, evil is aggressive and destructive. As a parasite on God's creation, evil takes on the characteristics of a kingdom—a kingdom of evil.

Dismissing evil as an illusion, in my opinion, exhibits a naive if not immoral insensitivity to the pain and suffering endured by people like Janice.

The Bible certainly doesn't treat evil as an illusion. Nowhere does the Bible simply urge captives, exiles, and others who suffer to deny the reality of their condition. Instead, the Bible calls for a Redeemer powerful enough to break the chains of oppression and set the captive free. The Bible presents the God who is resourceful enough to overcome evil and restore peace.

Another of the larger weeds is the belief that there are two sources of being or existence instead of one, as monotheism claims. This attempted solution is called "metaphysical dualism," because it claims there are two ultimate and opposed sources of being. From one source of existence comes all that is evil. From the other source comes all that is good. Third-century gnosticism, which threatened at times to undermine Christianity, was dualistic in this sense.

As you might already know, before Augustine became a Christian, he was part of a dualistic religious group called the Manichaeans. You may recall that the Manichaeans believed that two independent and opposing principles govern the universe. To one source we should attribute evil. To the other we should attribute good.

At first, dualism seemed to satisfy Augustine's questions about the origin of evil. Eventually, however, he saw the impossibility of two absolutes.

Today, many Christians function this way even if they don't verbalize it. They often speak as if the devil is a reality quite independent of God. Christians who speak this way make it sound as though the devil provides his own source of being. Of course, according to the Bible, this should be said of God alone. But Christian dualists, who are many in number, think that the devil is just a little shy of being as powerful as God. If you were to point to the implications of their dualistic solution, they would probably quickly back away.

According to dualism, evil should be blamed solely on matter, flesh, earthly existence, and an evil being who is the source of it all. Hope for overcoming evil resides in the belief that someday spirit will be set free from this evil world. There is no reason to hope that the physical world will ever be redeemed.

As you can see, Barbara, metaphysical dualism seems to be attractive in some ways. It seems to provide tidy answers regarding the source of evil and the reason for its continuation.

Most attractive of all, dualism seems to release God from any responsibility for evil. When a moral outrage such as the New York City attacks occurs, dualists can say with accuracy, "Hey! Don't look at God. He didn't do it. He wasn't there. Put the blame where it should be, on the powerful source of all evil."

Another reason this solution appeals to many is that it relaxes human responsibility, especially when flesh is rigidly associated with the devil, and spirit with God. Such a solution produces what is sometimes called the Flip Wilson solution—"the devil made me do it!"

Dualism and the monotheistic faith of the Bible are mutually exclusive. According to the Bible, no power great or small is independent of God. "To whom then will you compare me, that I should be like him? says the Holy One" (Isa. 40:25). The anticipated answer is "No one!" God sets the boundaries for all things, and nothing successfully places boundaries on Him.

Dualism directly contradicts the Bible's claim that God alone is the Creator and that all He created was good. Dualism repudiates the Bible's affirmation that God can employ even the otherwise mundane parts of creation to declare His glory. If dualism were true, then the manger, the Cross, and Christian sacraments would have to be abandoned. We would also have to abandon the promise in Rom. 8 that the whole creation is being redeemed. Neither could Col. 1:15-21 be true.

The next of the larger weeds gives the appearance of being more difficult to handle. Numerous people solve the problem of evil by saying that God is necessarily finite and that consequently His ability to impact human and world affairs is inescapably limited. No matter how great God is, a surplus of evil just continues to seep out. No more should be expected of an all-loving, but finite, God. Filmmaker Woody Allen said, "About the worst thing you can say about God is that He is an underachiever."

The argument goes something like this: "God is doing the best He can, so for Pete's sake get off His back." Not that God willingly limits himself, but that He is inherently limited. Like the rest of us, God, too, lives within fixed limits over which He has no control. He is powerful but not all-powerful.

Many adopt this or a similar position. I mentioned in my October 23 letter that Rabbi Harold Kushner does this in *When Bad Things Happen to Good People*. You may recall that I also spoke there of God's self-imposed vulnerability. It is not the same thing. The vulnerability of divine love should never be confused with divine finitude. To the contrary, as we saw earlier, the vulnerability of God's love discloses His sovereignty.

Attempts to solve the problem of evil by setting forth a finite God are clumsy and dishonest. If God is finite, then evil ceases to be a religious problem. Only if God is both all-powerful and all-loving can protests against Him, because of evil, have any meaning at all. If God were necessarily finite, then we would be foolish to expect anything more.

Well, Barbara, as is usually the case, this job took more effort and time than I expected. Having now cleared away the weeds, I think it is time for a rest. Tonight I'll go to the Citadel, where the Marine Band from Parris Island will present a concert. I wouldn't miss it.

I will be deeply disappointed if you cannot come to Charleston this winter. But if you must postpone your visit, I will understand. I am continuing to make plans for your time here.

I pray peace and strength for you.

Uncle Carl

9

Saturday, November 10, 2001
Charleston, South Carolina

Dear Barbara,

I hope this letter reaches you before you attempt to answer my November 8 letter. As I mentioned at the close of that letter, on Thursday evening I went to the Citadel to hear the Parris Island Marine Band. The band was excellent. For me, the band majored on the perfect combination: Jimmy Dorsey and John Philip Sousa. What more could one want from a concert?

While I sat listening to the music, I remembered that in Monday's letter I left out one very popular and seemingly inextinguishable "resolution" for the problem of moral evil. I don't know how I could have overlooked it.

Many people believe that human suffering is punishment for wrongdoing. This is an ancient and universal explanation that finds reception in most of the world's religions, including Christianity. I shall never forget listening to a Sikh calmly explain why four children died on a cold winter's day in a Chicago house fire. The death had shaken most of us who had heard about it. But the Sikh said, "The children must have committed horrible crimes in their previous lives. Their karma was just working itself out." Minus the idea of reincarnation, many Christians can be heard saying pretty much the same.

On the surface, this "resolution" holds sweeping explanatory powers. It rests on a simple cause-and-effect formula. It also relies heavily on belief that God directly punishes people for wrongs they do and that His computer doesn't malfunction. When someone suffers, God is either punishing them, cultivating their obedience, or just trying to get their attention.

The idea that suffering results from evils done shows up in the Old Testament. Supposedly the evil suffer and the righteous flourish. When people commit wrongs, punishment will be visited not only upon the offender but also "upon the children and the children's children, to the third and the fourth generation" (Exod. 34:7).

One of the earliest and boldest statements of this idea, and one of the strongest arguments against it, occur in the Book of Job. Job knew that his calamitous anguish was not the result of wrongdoing. But he could not convince anyone else of this. Eliphaz, Job's first "comforter," states the doctrine of punishment in the form of a question. He asks, "Think now, who that was innocent ever perished? Or where were the upright cut off?" (Job 4:7). Eliphaz says that based upon his own observations, he can confirm the doctrine of this-worldly, divine retribution: "As I have seen, those who plow iniquity and sow trouble reap the same" (v. 8). Eliphaz is confident that the righteous do not suffer as Job is suffering. Only wicked people suffer.

When we move into the New Testament, the belief that suffering is the direct result of evils committed is still prominent. One clear illustration shows up in Jesus' disciples. Once, as they passed by a blind man, they asked Jesus, "Rabbi, who sinned, this man or his parents, that he was born blind?" (John 9:2). Jesus answered, "Neither."

This explanation finds a prominent place in C. S. Lewis's efforts to deal with human suffering. Evil, he says, is God's way of getting our attention: "God whispers to us in our pleasures, speaks in our conscience, but shouts in our pains: it is His megaphone to rouse a deaf world." This explanation quickly showed up in New York City as people tried to make sense of the September 11 destruction and suffering.

Recently a friend E-mailed to me an article from the Internet. Somebody named Kimberly Southall was writing. She said that nearly two months after the explosion, in scores of conversations, people were saying that if God permitted this unparalleled act of domestic terror, then He must have been trying to send a message to New York City. She was speculating that He might be sending a wake-up call so people would turn to Him, punishing us for forgetting Him. Southall added that God chose September 11 for His discipline as His way of saying we have an emergency and had better call His 9-1-1 for help.

For me and for many others, one of the most riveting statements of the notion that suffering is punishment for sin comes from Father Paneloux. I mentioned him in my letter two days ago as the Jesuit priest in Albert Camus's novel *The Plague*. Barbara, you know more about Camus than I will ever know. I hope that you will be patient with an amateur's treatment of the book.

You will remember that Father Paneloux was known in the city of Oran as a stalwart champion of Christian doctrine in its "most precise and purest" form. In his order, he was also a respected scholar.

[**A note to the reader:** Because Barbara is a professor of literature, the following setting for *The Plague* was missing from the original letter. For those who might not know the story, the setting is briefly added here: *The Plague* tells of an outbreak of bubonic plague in an Algerian port city named Oran. No one in the city wanted to believe that in the early 1940s such an ancient and dreaded menace could strike a modern city. But as the symptoms increased, and as the death toll mounted, all doubt was erased. Camus's descriptions of the symptoms and the deaths of plague victims are horrific and soul-wrenching. The plague was no respecter of persons. Children and adults were caught in its grip.

[As the plague intensified, the ecclesiastical authorities in the town decided to do battle against it by organizing a Week of Prayer. This manifestation of public piety was to conclude on Sunday with a high mass. Father Paneloux would deliver the sermon. He was a stockily built man, of medium height, who wore big round glasses.]

Dr. Rieux, the narrator of the story, notes that the people of Oran were not particularly devout, but large crowds attended the services of the Week of Prayer anyway. I chuckle over the attitude of many of them: "It can't do any harm."

On Sunday the cathedral was full. When Father Paneloux rose to deliver the sermon, he leaned on the edge of the pulpit and grasped the woodwork with his big hands. In clear, emphatic tones, he began: "Calamity has come on you, my brethren, and, my brethren, you deserved it. . . . From the dawn of recorded history the scourge of God has humbled the proud of heart and laid low those who hardened themselves against Him. Ponder this well, my friends, and fall on your knees." Presently, everyone had slipped forward from their seats and onto their knees.

The sermon continued: "If today the plague is in your midst, that is because the hour has struck for taking thought. The just man need have no fear, but the evildoer has good cause to tremble. For plague is the flail of God and the world His threshing-floor." According to the preacher, God did not will the plague. But because of the sins of the city, His judgment had fallen. He had grown weary of waiting for the people to repent. He had wanted the people to do more than just come to church on Sundays and "bend a knee." God had judged their indifference as "criminal."

God had loosed His visitation—the plague—on Oran. "Now you are learning your lesson, the lesson that was learned by Cain and his offspring, by the people of Sodom and Gomorrah, by Job and Pharaoh, by all that hardened their hearts against Him."

Does Paneloux offer the people any good news? Yes, according to his theology. First he makes it clear that the plague came from God to punish the people's sins. Then he offers "hope": "And thus my brothers, at last it is revealed to you, the divine compassion which has ordained good and evil in everything; wrath and pity; the plague and your salvation. This same pestilence which is slaying you works for your good and points your path."

But where is the word of hope? The answer? God is using the plague to bring the people to repentance and salvation. He is "unfailingly transforming evil into good." He is leading the sinners through the dark valley of fears and groans toward . . . the wellspring of all life.

Paneloux concluded his sermon by praying that despite all the horrors of "these dark days," the congregants would offer up to heaven a prayer of love for God.

In the days ahead, Paneloux's theology will unravel like a cheap rope. Because he believes that the plague is the direct activity of God, he has no theological permission to work with the doctors who are trying to relieve the suffering. In his first sermon, Father Paneloux had warned that no one should seek "to force God's hand or hurry on . . . the order of events which God has ordained unalterably." By the priest's theology, anyone who attempts to relieve the ravages of plague, or develop a serum, is fighting against God. On the other hand, the medical doctors are acting more like the compassionate

Christ, who healed the sick, than is Father Paneloux. But, given his explanation for human suffering, he is trapped.

Eventually, the priest does join Dr. Rieux. But he has no way to explain why he assists in relieving suffering. He tells his congregants, "This is a hard lesson for us all; we must convince ourselves that there is no island of escape in time of plague. No, there is no middle course. We must accept the dilemma and choose either to hate God or to love God. And who would dare to choose to hate Him . . . my brothers?" Paneloux concluded, "The love of God is a hard love. . . . It alone can reconcile us to suffering and the deaths of children."

The unraveling of Paneloux's explanation continued. He had absolutely no way to explain why the plague was so indiscriminate. Why were innocent children dying? Their death scenes were among the most grotesque of all. The priest could not bring himself to apply his theology to the little children. But if he could not, then his explanation for the plague would collapse. Also, while mutilating children, the plague skipped over some of the most infamous sinners in the town.

The collapse of Paneloux's explanation for suffering was made complete when he himself became a plague victim. Clearly, according to the first sermon, Paneloux thought that he was among the innocent. From his own mouth had come the promise—as must be true for this explanation of evil—"The just man need have no fear, but the evildoer has good cause to tremble."

Paneloux's death is the worst of all, not because the symptoms are more grotesque, but because his death is the most meaningless. His entire explanation for suffering has been contradicted. At his own death, he can't utter one intelligible explanation. Nevertheless Paneloux dies loving what he cannot understand.

Barbara, I have given considerable time to this "explanation" for evil, not because it is so convincing, but because it is so tenaciously popular. I am not naive. Having been a parish minister for many years, I know all too well what can happen to persons when they ignore moral and health responsibilities. Many times I have stood by the bedsides of persons whose lungs had been destroyed by cigarettes. I have ministered to persons whose bodies were mangled because they tried to drive while intoxicated. But never did I quote Father Paneloux to any of them. Nor would I let them blame their tragedies on God, even though people often tried to do so.

To those who so freely use Father Paneloux's "explanation" for human suffering, even if well intended, I say, "Go stand at the gaping, jagged hole where the Trade Centers once stood. Stand there while rescuer George Healey, choking back tears, helps bring out the mutilated body parts of the victims. Then, if you dare, repeat your 'explanation' to the families of the victims when you confirm the deaths of their loved ones."

I remember a statement by Friedrich Nietzsche, the German philosopher that some preachers enjoy banging around. Nietzsche said that one reason he had trouble believing that Christians really embrace the gospel of Christ is because they hold so tenaciously to the hope that God will finally act vindictively against all their enemies.

There are numerous good reasons for rejecting Eliphaz and Paneloux. I have already identified three by showing how, in the midst of plague, Paneloux's explanation slowly collapsed. But the two strongest reasons have not been given.

The first of the two reasons for rejecting the notion that suffering is the flail of God's wrath on impenitent sinners is because Jesus Christ said God is not like that at all. If Jesus has the authority to speak for God, as the Christian faith claims, then Paneloux, Eliphaz, Jesus' disciples (John 9), and the men who wanted to kill the women taken in adultery (8:3-11) are wrong—just plain wrong.

One reason Jesus ran afoul of the ecclesiastical authorities was that He disagreed with an explanation of evil similar to Paneloux's. Worse, He said that He was speaking for His Heavenly Father. How do we know Jesus disagreed with the orthodox explanation for evil? Because He repeatedly healed, fed, and loved people whom the authorities thought were receiving their just punishments from God. At the most fundamental level, He challenged the orthodox way of explaining God's relationship to evil.

Listen to Jesus' refutation of Eliphaz and Paneloux:

If you love those who love you, what credit is that to you? For even sinners love those who love them. And if you do good to those who do good to you, what credit is that to you? For even sinners do the same. . . . But love your enemies, and do good, and lend, expecting nothing in return; and your reward will be great, and you will be sons of the Most High; for he is kind to the ungrateful and the selfish. Be merciful, even as your Father is merciful (Luke 6:32-33, 35-36).

There's a wideness in God's mercy
Like the wideness of the sea;
There's a kindness in His justice
Which is more than liberty.
—Frederick W. Faber

In the presence of human suffering, the choice is not, as Father Paneloux thought, between hating God or loving Him. The choice is between Jesus' testimony to the character of God and Paneloux's testimony.

Finally, the cross of Jesus Christ is the second of the strongest reasons for rejecting this explanation. Had Paneloux—and the host of his ancient and contemporary supporters—been correct, then plague, not the gospel, would have been God's last word. But the God who meets us in the Cross is not a punitive calculator of wrongs done and punishments administered. Instead, He is like Jesus of Nazareth, who welcomed prodigals, gave new life to adulterers, sought lost sheep, and went home with Zacchaeus for lunch. The apostle Paul said it well: "God shows his love for us in that while we were yet sinners Christ died for us" (Rom. 5:8).

Barbara, in this letter there is one aspect of God to which I have not given attention. In both the Old and the New Testaments we meet the wrath of God. Any concept of God that ignores His wrath thereby fails to deal adequately with the God of the Bible.

Honestly, Barbara, I find it difficult to understand the wrath of God. I find it even more difficult to discuss. But this much I do know —while the Bible says repeatedly that God is love, it never says that God is wrath. Whatever the wrath of God is, His love defines it and governs it. It is a wrath that always serves love's ends. Look at the message in Isa. 57:15-19 that God addressed to the exiles.

The wrath of God must be seen in light of what we know about God through Jesus Christ. We believe that God is like Jesus. Because of the cross of our Lord, we know that God has dealt mercifully and graciously with us, not according to our sins.

Someone has correctly said that the wrath of God is "wounded divine love." Its purpose is redemptive, not vindictive. Pointless punishment and love are contradictory concepts.

I am amazed by how often, and how thoughtlessly, some Christians divorce God's wrath from His love. When they do, they represent a deity other than the Father of our Lord and Savior Jesus Christ. In Jesus we meet the God of suffering love. Unlike Father Paneloux, God is "in the streets with the victims of plague." His suffering love places Him there.

The September 24, 2001, issue of *U.S. News & World Report* relayed a story that has become for me a parable of God. After the Pentagon was struck by Flight 77, a secretary was in shock and could not move. She was in danger of being engulfed by fire. A young soldier hoisted her onto his back and carried her across a wall to safety.

"You never leave somebody behind," a nearby colonel commented (42). Does God do anything less?

Barbara, I am praying that my letters will promote healing in Janice and cultivate faith in her. I will look forward to your next letter with anticipation.

I send my love to you and Janice.

With deepest love,
Uncle Carl

10

Tuesday, November 20, 2001
New York City

Dear Uncle Carl,

Janice and I are still reeling from the challenge you presented in your two recent letters. So far, you have dismissed all those who want to rush God away from the scene of the crime. We hope that before this discussion is over, some candidate will offer a dependable solution to the reality of evil. As a matter of fact, Janice and I think we have a solution you will approve.

You have certainly won Janice's respect by being so honest with us. She says that you have already discredited some of the explanations well-meaning folk have offered her.

Well, rule out the January trip to Charleston. The condition of Virginia's husband has worsened. She cannot leave the city. So I will be going to Dallas during the time Janice and I hoped to be in Charleston. However, if you agree, we will plan to come in March during my spring break. Since Janice's schedule is more flexible than mine, March will work for her as well. I remember how beautiful Charleston can be in March. So I am not terribly disappointed.

At the suggestion of our minister, Janice has begun sessions with a counselor. Until recently, she has gotten along fairly well during the day while she is active. But the last few weeks she has been experiencing nightmares so disruptive that they diminish her energy during the day. Counselors are doing a thriving business in this city.

I had forgotten about your keen interest in Kafka and Camus. I will give you a good grade for the way you handled both of them. They are favorites of mine, largely because of their honesty.

Speaking of novels, I told you of the book I want to write. I continue to sketch the characters and the plot. But each letter I receive from you sends me scurrying back to the drawing board.

We have been talking to Jeff again. He gave us an explanation for the problem of evil known as the soul-making theodicy. He quickly added that "theodicy" means explaining the ways of God to humankind, particularly with regard to the problem of evil.

Later, after describing the soul-making explanation, Jeff provided some articles that added to our understanding. The soul-making explanation seems quite satisfying to us. But Jeff cautioned that it has some serious problems. He would not identify them. Instead, he said, "Let your uncle help you find them."

Now, if you were reluctant to discuss Albert Camus, Janice and I are hesitant to present soul-making to you. Be patient with our amateur efforts (as patient as you were with a little girl who put fig stains in your car).

Well, here goes. Based on what Jeff told us and on what we have read, the soul-making explanation for the reality of evil began with Irenaeus [**A note to the reader:** Irenaeus (c. 130—c. 202) was bishop of Lyons and a strong opponent of the gnostics, who threatened to subvert the faith of the Church], one of the Early Church fathers.

Irenaeus made an important distinction between God creating humankind in His image and His likeness. The image resides in humankind's physical form. It represents our nature as intelligent creatures who are capable of fellowship with God. The likeness represents humankind's final perfecting by the Holy Spirit.

A person can be created in the image of God and still fail to achieve His likeness. If a person doesn't allow the Holy Spirit to perfect him or her in God's likeness, he or she will remain carnal and imperfect.

According to John Hick, moral freedom and responsibility would be included in what Irenaeus meant by image. When created, Adam and Eve were only at the beginning of a process of growth and development in God's continuing providence. They were immature beings upon whom He could not profitably bestow His higher gifts. But along the way, He would continually transform them into His likeness.

Unlike what the traditional interpretation says, Adam and Eve's sin was not a damnable revolt. Instead, it called forth God's compassion in response to weakness and immaturity. God would teach Adam and Eve how to be His children and how to live in gratitude to Him.

Within the providences of God, humankind can make decisions for the good and against the evil. When the children of God fail to glorify Him, they can repent, recover, learn, and grow as a result. Both the good and the bad aspects of life are meant as opportunities for growing in God's likeness.

Obviously, many people do not grow in the likeness of God. Instead, they remain immature, and their bad choices can spawn immense evils in the world.

How are we doing, Uncle Carl?

According to Jeff, John Hick embraced and developed Irenaeus's ideas. He, too, distinguished two dimensions in God's creation of humankind. First, God created man as rational and responsible. Humankind had the potential for existing in conscious fellowship with Him. Second, being made in the likeness of God is not something that happens in a moment of creation. This takes a lifetime. It happens through uncompelled obedient responses to God. Growth in likeness occurs also through willing cooperation between human beings. By this process we become children of God in the New Testament sense. This is the process of "soul-making."

The "child of God in the making" meets and eventually masters evils and temptations. In the process, persons become good in a much richer and value-laden sense than if Adam and Eve had been created already perfect. The goodness that comes through the patient process of soul-making has within it the strength of temptations met and overcome. Responsible and virtuous character comes from investing costly personal effort in concrete challenges.

God desires to bring many daughters and sons to maturity (Heb. 2:10). Even the evils generated by terrorists and drive-by shootings present opportunities for achieving the likeness of God. True, this is a long and sometimes tortuous process, but the process of soul-making has value in the eyes of the Creator that justifies the long journey.

The danger that many people will badly miss God's purpose is the price that must be paid for being free to become mature persons in His likeness. To be free to engage in soul-making, we must also be free to bring suffering upon ourselves and others.

Uncle Carl, the immense evils in our world count not at all against God being all-powerful and all-loving. Instead, their presence actually declares His glory and wisdom. Look around, Hick tells us, and you will see a world in which humankind is being changed into the likeness of God by overcoming this world's evils. He writes:

God is so overwhelmingly great that the children in His heavenly family [are] prodigal children who have voluntarily come to their Father from a far country, prompted by their own need and drawn by His love. This means that the sinfulness from which man is being redeemed, and the human suffering which flows from that sinfulness, have in their own paradoxical way a place within the divine providence. Their place, however, is not that of something that ought to exist, but of something that ought to be abolished (John Hick, *Evil and the God of Love*, 323).

In a world custom-made for the avoidance of sin, pain, and suffering, much more would be lost than gained. If suffering and pain were absent, moral qualities would not develop. It would be a world without need for the virtues of self-sacrifice, care for others, devotion to the public good, courage, perseverance, and honesty. These values lose their significance in the absence of their opposites. Unselfishness would never emerge in a world where no one was ever in real need or danger.

Uncle Carl, Janice has a sermon in manuscript form preached by a New York City-area minister on September 23. It beautifully illustrates what Hick is describing. Here are a few statements from the sermon: "It was our [New York City] families who rejoiced with every person found alive, even before they knew the fate of their own family members. Nearby restaurants and stores brought food, and volunteers handed out water bottles." The sermon names incident after incident just as beautiful as these. All of the beautiful deeds the pastor names are instances of soul-making. The minister's wife, for example, stood in line for seven and a half hours to donate blood.

By contrast, just as John Hick predicted, where there are opportunities for soul-making, there is also an opportunity for soul degeneracy. Perhaps you heard the story of the man who called rescuers telling them he was calling from a cell phone and was trapped in the rubble. The rescuers expended valuable time and undertook dangerous steps to save the man who they later realized was playing a prank on them.

Uncle Carl, this lengthy letter pays you back for the "epistles" you have been writing. Janice and I hope that we have fairly represented Irenaeus and Hick. If not, correct us. At least you have the Thanksgiving holiday to think it over.

We think the soul-making explanation is convincing. Janice feels particularly good about it, especially in light of the outpouring of support and love given to the citizens of New York City from all over the world. We will look forward to your response.

My love to you,
Barbara

11

Monday, November 26, 2001
Charleston, South Carolina

Dear Barbara,

Since you and Janice can't come to South Carolina, I will bring you here by way of description. You would have enjoyed being with me on Monday. Another retired priest and I took his deck boat 25 miles up the Cooper River, up to Monk's Corner and the Old Santee Canal State Park. The trip took us past the Charleston Navy base, the Mepkin Abbey, and the remains of the colonial era rice plantations. In some places the old dikes and floodgates are still visible.

It doesn't take much imagination to envision the 1800s river traffic or to hear the sounds of plantation commerce. When you come, perhaps I can take you and Janice and the kids into that enchanted region.

My compliments go to you and Janice for your presentation of Irenaeus and John Hick. I think that both of them would be pleased with you.

I share much of your admiration for the soul-making solution to the problem of evil. It is one of the two or three most important efforts available for dealing with the problem of evil. John Hick does a splendid job of stating his position.

All of us know how the concrete fulfillment of values enriches human life, and we have observed how rejecting virtues and values causes life to decline. On September 11 emergency medical personnel and doctors saved many lives. Many of them rushed to the scene from their regular lives. The soul-making explanation just seems to comply with the way we experience life. In some small way, most of us go through this process each day.

However, just as Jeff warned you, there are major problems associated with the soul-making solution.

First, the language of Irenaeus was Greek. The two Greek words he used for image and likeness will support the distinction on which his ideas depend. But the Hebrew language simply will not support his distinction between image and likeness. In Hebrew, the two words are roughly synonyms. The Hebrew language often piles synonyms on top of each other for the purpose of enriching the text.

So the truth is that so far as the Old Testament is concerned, Irenaeus built his understanding of personhood on a linguistic error. Sorry, but this fact sort of stops the train in its tracks.

Even more can be said about the biblical accounts in Gen. 1:26-30 and 2:7-9. When we examine the two accounts of humankind's creation, there is no indication that there was a fundamental religious and moral deficit in Adam and Eve. The biblical record indicates that when God created them, He gave them all they needed to live in obedience to and in communion with Him. True, Adam and Eve were given an assignment in creation that would involve exercising values. But not one word is said about needing to overcome existing evils in order to fulfill their God-given mission.

Implicitly at least, the soul-making explanation demands that before humankind can choose for God, it must first assert itself against God. Soul-making necessarily puts God and humankind on a collision course. The Genesis accounts of creation reject this notion.

Next, I think this solution turns out to be something of a white elephant. It doesn't remove the problem of evil at all. Instead, in the name of complimenting a wise God who created a world in which soul-making can occur, it actually chains Him to evil. Study the argument closely, and you will see that for humankind to achieve the values that fulfill His divine design for likeness, the actuality of sin and evil—not just their possibility—are necessary. God cannot fulfill His purposes apart from evil and suffering. Evil becomes His Siamese twin. They share the same heart and cannot be separated without destroying both.

The problem can be stated even more strongly. In the soul-making solution, sin and evil actually become good—instrumentally good.

Let's use an illustration. If in order to perform a liver transplant in an infant, the surgeon must cut through the child's flesh, is the cutting good or bad? Obviously, the question has to be answered with reference to the intended good. Since cutting through the flesh is necessary to achieve the good, the cutting is instrumentally good.

If evil is necessary for soul-making, then evil—at least some of it—becomes instrumentally good. What kind of "solution" have we here?

Predictably, the soul-making solution to the problem of evil just won't work. Nothing in the two creation accounts indicates that God needs evil to accomplish His purposes. Judged by His instructions to Adam and Eve, such a notion is absurd. God makes it clear to Adam and Eve that, as created, the creation is good. Everything He planned for His creation could be accomplished in the absence of evil.

Furthermore, if to any extent sin and evil become necessary, the meaning of God's holiness and love become so compromised as to lose their significance. Worshiping a God who is necessarily allied with evil would, from the perspective of monotheism, be unthinkable.

Critics have also pointed out that Hick's solution does not treat sin as seriously as the Bible does. He seems to deny the reality of genuine evil. Given the instrumental goodness of at least some evil, it is not surprising that Hick's treatment of sin does not contain the urgent indignation against sin, idols, lies, and wicked error that we find in the Old Testament prophets. Hick seems not to shudder with horror as the prophets did over unbelief, rebellion, or spiritual infidelity.

Barbara, stay with me a little longer on this point. In the Bible, sin is not pictured primarily as a moral or aesthetic challenge. No, primarily sin is anarchy in God's universe. It is rebellion against Him. Although it is true that the soul-making explanation doesn't justify sin and evil, it does tend to minimize their catastrophic impact.

In one of my early letters, I said that we would have to reject any "solution" that diminishes either the sovereignty or love of God. I also said the same about evil and suffering. Perhaps without intending to, Hick does the latter by making evil inevitable and instrumentally good. The Bible will have none of this. In the Bible, God does not need evil's assistance, and evil is not inevitable. It contributes to no harmony or greater good in the universe. Evil is the creature's unjust, ungrateful, and senseless response to God. Nothing less. Sin is defined by its opposition to God, not by some secondary service to Him.

The Bible teaches that God is never the author of evil and never complies with it. Nor does He ever directly cause it but acts unfailingly to overcome it. A French theologian, Henri Blocher, says emphatically: "When the Bible's vision of sin and evil is contrasted with all ancient and modern pagan notions, the Bible displays unmistakable clarity."

Third, there is another problem with the soul-making explanation. Why are the opportunities for soul-making spread so unevenly? Some countries have far more opportunities for soul-making than others. For example, if the number of evils that need to be overcome provides any reliable measurement, the opportunities for soul-making in Rwanda and Bosnia are greater than they are in Canada and Denmark. Why would God distribute the opportunities so unevenly? Does God love Rwandans more than Danes? We could also ask, why aren't folk rushing to places where opportunities for soul-making abound?

Fourth, the soul-making defense is supposed to demonstrate that in a world without suffering there would be no occasion for producing virtues such as courage, sympathy, forgiveness, and the like. But even if this were true, there is suffering far in excess of what is needed to produce virtue. A bank teller could learn forgiveness through an unkind customer. Is it necessary for her to suffer a gunshot wound in an armed robbery?

We know that there are other ways to produce virtue. A father who regularly and patiently helps a fourth grader learn math is both teaching and learning patience, fortitude, and strength of character in the absence of evil. The same can be said for a parent who cares for a sick child.

Finally, soul-making is a self-contradictory concept. And if it is self-contradictory, then soul-making is worthless as a solution. Supposedly, in the process of soul-making, humans should be overcoming the things that cause evil. In the interest of maximizing values, we should be eliminating diseases, wars, racism, exploitation of one class by another, hunger, and so on. The idea of soul-making rests largely on the belief that this can be done.

But wait a minute. If we succeed, we will cheat future generations out of their opportunities to grow their souls! That would be wrong. But if we don't try to succeed, we will become slothful and even more sinful. Neither option is morally acceptable. Logically, soul-making is impossible. And if it is impossible, then obviously it is not acceptable as a solution to the problem of evil.

To save the soul-making explanation, we could do what Hick does in one presentation of his ideas. We could appeal to modern evolutionary theory and talk about the long ascending march of humankind. We could say that through the evolutionary process, God has been "bringing many daughters and sons to maturity." In the history of the evolutionary march, we could say there have been many obstacles to overcome. Each time an obstacle such as deadly diseases, or the organization of societies, has been overcome, evolution of the human spirit has advanced. Soul-making, one could argue, fits better into the modern temperament than does the Genesis pictures of humankind's creation.

Whatever the merits or demerits of evolutionary theory might be, no one can miss the fact that if we accept Hick's "scientific explanation," then the basis on which the soul-making explanation stands has changed dramatically. No longer are we appealing to the Bible for theological support and explanation. The locus of authority is now modern evolutionary theory. One simply cannot make this change and at the same time claim to serve the biblical text when accounting for the reality of moral evil.

There is another major weakness in the soul-making explanation for the reality of evil. But I want to expose it when in another letter we look at "the free will defense."

Barbara, I am sorry to disappoint your hopes regarding soul-making as a satisfactory explanation for evil. But as some folk say in this part of the South, "This dog just won't hunt!" We will have to wait for something better, if it exists.

Next Sunday I will travel 60 miles up the coast to Georgetown. I will be the guest celebrant and preacher in Prince George Episcopal Church. The church was founded in 1721 and named in honor of George II, who reigned as king of England from 1727 to 1760.

You, Janice, and the citizens of New York City and Washington will be mentioned specifically when prayers are offered in Prince George next Sunday.

With love,
Uncle Carl

12

Wednesday, December 5, 2001
New York City

Dear Uncle Carl,

Janice and I will hold you to your offer. As you probably intended, your brief description of your trip up the Cooper River made us want to go along. Janice said that she once saw an intriguing PBS film that traced the history of that part of the Lowcountry. She remembers vaguely that the old Santee Canal was more a technical than a financial success.

Our schedules will allow us to come to Charleston the end of the third week in March and probably stay until the 30th. Will these dates fit into your schedule?

Wow! Your critique of soul-making almost blew us away. We thought we had found a fairly reliable answer to our questions. We showed your letter to Jeff. He actually chuckled as he read. When finished, he said, "In my opinion, your uncle hit the bull's-eye." He even complimented you by saying that you had noted a couple of objections new to him.

Jeff asked us if we had discussed the "free will defense" with you, and I told him you'd mentioned it in passing. He said that it is probably the most popular explanation of all. By his estimate, when stated correctly, it is probably the strongest attempt to resolve the problem of evil. Jeff says that some very big names are associated with it, among them Augustine and Thomas Aquinas. That captured our attention. Jeff offered to help us formulate the position so that we could discuss it with you. Janice needled him by asking, "Jeff, why didn't you give this one to us first?" "You needed an opportunity for soul-making," he answered.

After more conversations with Jeff (we had to feed him first), Janice and I want to present the free will defense for your consideration. We find it attractive. We should also tell you that Jeff has edited our presentation. See if Janice and I understand the free will defense correctly.

When God created humankind, He intended to create a being who could actually engage in willful, loving, and fruitful relationship with Him. God could have created a puppet and called him Adam if He had wanted to. Without fail, the perfect puppet would have responded in exact compliance with divine instructions. However, creating "man" in this way would have come at the expense of a mutually enriching, loving relationship between God and humankind.

Remove finite freedom, and the word love—at least at the human level—loses all meaning. Coercion and love are mutually exclusive terms.

Jeff has advised us to use the phrase "finite freedom" when speaking of human freedom. No creature has absolute freedom. Human freedom is always limited in some way. All of us are to some extent limited by time, space, family background, native gifts, and so on. Within our individual limitations we become the particular persons we are.

When creating humankind, God actually created a junior partner who was to be His chief representative and responsible steward in the world. Only of humankind does Genesis say, "So God created man in his own image, in the image of God he created him" (1:27). God made Adam a steward—a highly responsible position—over the creation. Doing so would involve the exercise of advanced freedom.

I am reminded of the majestic words in Ps. 8 that expand in poetic form God's words in Genesis:

> What is man that thou art mindful of him,
>> and the son of man that thou dost care for him?
> Yet thou hast made him little less than God,
>> and dost crown him with glory and honor.
> Thou hast given him dominion over the works
>> of thy hands;
> thou hast put all things under his feet.
>
> (vv. 4-6)

According to Jeff, we have completed the first step in the free will defense.

The second step is that God can do nothing that implies contradiction. To attach "God" to a self-contradictory statement doesn't all of a sudden make it self-consistent. Nonsense remains nonsense. Jeff used as an example "a wall so high no one can jump it." If that is the nature of the wall, then it makes no sense to ask, "Can God jump it?" Or, if an object is square, even God can't make it round. Otherwise, it would no longer be a square.

Now, step three. Real freedom to choose the good and all that is excellent necessarily includes real freedom to choose evil and all that is degenerative. The possibility of choosing great values necessarily includes freedom to choose disvalue.

A world where the absence of evil is assured will also be one where worship of God and moral excellence are absent. C. S. Lewis commented that if we exclude the possibility of suffering and evil from finite freedom, we succeed only in excluding human life itself.

To speak of creatures who have freedom to choose the good, but who do not have freedom to choose evil, is nonsense. When God created humankind, He set in motion magnificent possibilities for exercising human freedom. But in so doing, He also set in motion the possibility that humankind would badly miss the divine vocation.

Those who think that the reality of evil presents a major obstacle to confidence in an all-loving and all-powerful God should examine themselves, not God. They are the ones with a problem—a problem of elementary reasoning.

Jeff gave to us a statement by a Christian philosopher named Alvin Plantinga that seems to fit here: "God can create free creatures, but He can't cause or determine them to do what is right. . . . To create creatures capable of moral good, therefore, He must create creatures capable of moral evil."

[**A note to the reader:** By an impressive and well-known use of logic, Christian philosopher Alvin Plantinga has shown how evil can be made compatible with God's existence. But most of his supporters and critics agree that he has not succeeded in showing how the reality of evil can be made compatible with a God who is all-loving and all-powerful. In fact, Plantinga did not aim at resolving the problem of evil. Because he did not, his masterful use of logic is of no help to those of us who want to know how the reality of evil can be reconciled with the God who is supposedly all-loving and all-powerful.]

Much of the Bible traces the story of how humankind has often used its freedom to oppose God. The Bible tells the bitter story of what happens to nations, cultures, families, and persons when through the abuse of freedom sin enters. And enter it did.

The Bible is barely through telling the story of divine creation before Adam and Eve choose to do precisely what God had warned them not to do. Sin and evil have followed the pattern of that rebellion ever since.

Sin and evil that arise from an abuse of freedom amount to a civil war in God's good creation. Sin and evil are inexcusable. Neither their origin nor their consequences should be blamed on the Creator.

The Bible—especially the prophets—says that evil comes through the misuse of created freedom. Evil is linked primarily to the will and the heart as the faculty of choice. Isaiah points an accusing finger at the abuse of human freedom:

When I called, you did not answer,
when I spoke, you did not listen,
but you did what was evil in my eyes,
and chose what I did not delight in.
(65:12; cf. 66:4)

Zechariah also places the blame for evil on the misuse of the will: "They refused to hearken, and turned a stubborn shoulder, and stopped their ears that they might not hear" (7:11-12). Jesus wept over the evil will of Jerusalem that refused to be gathered to its Redeemer: "You would not!" (Matt. 23:37-38). As you know, Uncle Carl, the illustrations could be multiplied.

Jeff made a point that Janice understood more quickly than I. He said that when presenting the free will defense, we should not speak as though some power external to God imposed limitations on Him. Human freedom doesn't result from God's weakness. Instead, God freely bestows freedom. He freely limits himself in the interest of covenant.

Earlier you said that God's self-chosen vulnerability is clearly demonstrated in His creation of humankind. And along with creating humankind come the risks associated with finite freedom.

God did not create a world in which there is evil. But He did create a world in which, through the abuse of freedom, evil could occur. The initiative rests with Him.

Properly clarified, according to the free will defense, not even the most horrendous moral evils count against God's love and power. Anyone should see that He is in no sense implicated in the evils of this world. He created a good world, and sin entered through abused freedom.

Uncle Carl, Jeff says there is one more important part to the free will defense. There are diverse ranges or levels of freedom in the creation. By way of analogy, we can say that an elephant has more freedom than an amoeba. Therefore, it can achieve more complex values. For example, an elephant can entertain a circus audience in a way that the single-celled amoeba can't. But persons have the greatest degree of freedom and can achieve the most complex range of values. They can commune with God, create and perform great music, and build hospitals for those who are ill. They can engage in the innumerable acts of heroism and compassion shown in the aftermath of the New York City attack. Lenny Hatton, for example, gave his own life to save numbers of people in one of the buildings. Upon seeing him walk back toward the devastation, one of the persons Lenny had just saved asked, "Where are you going?" Lenny replied, "Back into the building." Lenny has not been seen since that moment.

However, along with the possibility for complex values comes the possibility for complex evils. As the scale of one rises, so does the other. Those who want real possibilities for developing complex values must realize that along with them comes an equally complex possibility for greed, selfishness, and exploitation.

The New York City attack illustrates this well. Along with the intelligence to create enormous airplanes that can fly hundreds of people tremendous distances comes the intelligence to turn that same airplane into a weapon of mass destruction, obliterating buildings and their occupants. Possibility for value is matched by possibility for disvalue. We can't eliminate one without eliminating the other.

Uncle Carl, now we can conclude. Place the blame for evil directly where it belongs—upon the abuse of finite freedom by humankind and Satan. God neither willed evil nor caused it.

Uncle Carl, we think we have found a winner. Do you agree?

The Advent season has taken on a distinct meaning because of September 11.

His peace,
Barbara

13

Wednesday, December 12, 2001
Charleston, South Carolina

Dear Barbara and Janice,

Greetings. I hope that in your church you are celebrating this particular Advent season in recognition that Christ is the hope of the world.

Since both of you worked on the December 5 letter, I think that I should address both of you.

I am delighted that you have set the dates for coming to Charleston. They fit well into my schedule. In fact, most dates do! The much-anticipated annual "Family Easter Concert" performed by the Charleston Symphony will be Sunday, March 24th.

I fully understand why you find the free will defense to be highly attractive. So did I. If one believes that God is all-loving and all-powerful, then this is the strongest available rational explanation.

I was impressed by the fact that Jeff recognizes the importance of saying that any limitations associated with God are those He willingly places upon himself. All too often, when the free will defense is presented, God's sovereignty evaporates into talk about "necessary" limitations on God. This morning I read Ps. 135. Verses 3-21 celebrate His freedom.

Janice and Barbara, when back in September you asked me to discuss the problem of evil, you demanded that I be an honest dialogue partner. I assume that your request still holds, even when dealing with the free will defense.

One question that must be asked of any alleged explanation of evil is, does it successfully maintain the twin affirmations that God is all-loving and all-powerful? Also, does the defense maintain His holiness? To succeed, a defense must be conceptually consistent. After careful scrutiny, any successful answer for evil must command the respect of an honest mind, no matter how cherished an argument might be. If in order to keep an explanation afloat, one has to ask the mind to overlook gaps in the argument, then success should not be claimed. This is true even if there is nothing better to take its place.

When judged by these standards, I am afraid that the free will defense fails the test. If we are looking for a rationally and morally satisfying explanation of how God and evil can exist at the same time, then the free will defense must withdraw its candidacy.

First, let me clear away a bit of clutter.

Often, those who critique the free will defense say that if God had known how humankind would abuse finite freedom, He would have had a moral responsibility not to create as He did. I have heard defenders of the free will defense respond, "But God did not know that humankind would abuse finite freedom. He gave finite freedom to humankind as a marvelous gift. From then on, how the gift would be used was completely humankind's responsibility."

This is one of the flimsiest responses to a criticism I have ever heard. I sometimes want to ask the speaker, "Do you want to be taken seriously, or are you just playing games with me?" Doesn't it contradict the claim that God is omniscient (all-knowing) to say that He didn't know humankind would abuse finite freedom? If God did not know that Adam and Eve would sin, then the future is as closed to Him as it is to us. Doesn't this desperate move "save" God by seriously diminishing Him?

Even if we were to allow the point, there would have been at least an extremely high likelihood that at some point humankind would abuse finite freedom and introduce evil into the world. God didn't just run a low risk that people might choose evil rather than good. Given the extremely high degree of probability, which even a finite mind could have predicted, can God really be declared completely free of responsibility for humankind's unleashing evil?

Let's say that a father gave his son a rifle that could be used for hunting wild game. But given the circumstances surrounding the son's use of the rifle, the father knew in advance that at some point the son would very likely use the rifle to kill someone. If you were on a jury after a murder had occurred, would you agree that none of the blame for the killing should be placed on the father?

Now let's discuss some of the major reasons given for rejecting the free will defense.

First, look at one of the consequences of saying that moral evil and suffering result from the abuse of freedom. A basic moral requirement must be met for this argument to succeed. Otherwise, God will look like a cosmic bungler. The requirement is that the consequences for abusing freedom must fall principally, if not exclusively, on those who abuse freedom. Consequences should be carefully allocated to the abuser. Otherwise, God has set in place a world in which unjust consequences are so randomly scattered they make Him appear irresponsible, if not immoral.

Janice and Barbara, what would you think of a judge who sentenced all members of a family to life in prison because one son living in a distant state murdered a clerk in a convenience store? Why excuse a God who allows an even more indiscriminate distribution of consequences? Is it sufficient for the judge to explain, "Well, first you have to understand the seriousness of the crime"? Maybe the judge could say, "You must understand the solidarity of the family. We can't just single out one family member to bear punishment for the crime. Once the crime was committed, punishment spread to the entire family." Would either of you agree with the judge?

If the consequences of abusing freedom could fall squarely on the abusers of freedom, then maybe the precise calculation would allow us to make moral sense of God's relationship to evil. But as the New York City attack so gruesomely illustrates, this is not the case. The consequences of the terrorist act fell on thousands of people who had done absolutely nothing to invite such lunacy.

The consequences of Adolf Hitler's evils fell on millions of people totally uninvolved in the Nazi schemes. For years I have kept a page from a seminary student's report to me on community service he was doing in a Salvation Army shelter for children. He told of a four-year-old child singing while riding a rocking horse. The child sang, "My real daddy, not my foster daddy, and my real mommy. My daddy stole money from my mom. He pushed her against the wall, and her head cracked. She bleeded." My student told me, "I will never forget that song!"

Now let's move to another criticism of the free will defense. Why is it that the opportunities for using freedom properly are so unevenly distributed? Many people have very little chance to exercise freedom in a morally creative way. Some people are poorly equipped and ill trained for the responsibility for freedom placed on them. A few succeed and learn. But the numbers seem not to be very many, given the world's population.

Some people are reared in circumstances calculated to produce moral cripples. How much should be expected of a child reared by a mother who is a prostitute and a crack cocaine addict? Is it sufficient simply to distribute evenly the blame and consequences? Is moral freedom evenly distributed? If not, can we honestly shift all of the blame for evil onto "free moral agents"? Some free will defenders answer that after Adam and Eve sinned, the perfect equilibrium was lost.

Next, Janice and Barbara, let's agree for a moment with the free will defense that evil flows from the abuse of finite freedom. God could not have established one and denied the other. Freedom to do evil is simply the flip side of the freedom to do good.

However, Jews and Christians believe that God has at times acted in history to moderate or even interrupt the consequences of abused freedom. Did His doing so damage some divine moral or natural order? If it did, then that presents a problem for Him. But if doing so did not damage the moral order, then what could possibly stand in the way of an all-loving, all-powerful God doing it all the time? If some divine efforts to moderate the consequences of freedom's abuse evoke in us praise and worship, wouldn't divine consistency in this manner of acting increase our opportunities for worship?

Let's put the matter somewhat differently. According to reports, God miraculously delivered some people from the doom of the World Trade Center. Allegedly, He even protected some people by keeping them away from the buildings on September 11. If this is true, could He not have quietly caused a heart attack for the terrorists days before the blast? No one would have ever known the difference, and surely no great damage to the moral order would have occurred.

Even if God doesn't eliminate all evil, given the fact that He is all-powerful and all-loving, doesn't He have a responsibility to nip in the bud major disasters such as the New York City or Pentagon tragedies? Couldn't He have caused Hitler to have a fatal heart attack in 1931? Who would have ever charged Him with acting too arbitrarily?

Often, in the face of such questions, defenders of the free will position flee to "holy ignorance." Almost angrily they will say, "We don't understand God's ways. You are foolish to raise such questions of Him."

Now honestly, if a person resorts to this shelter after having talked about all the miraculous things God has done, does he or she not invite ridicule? Are flights from rational responsibility more acceptable when done in God's name? If a person wishes to resort to this shelter, doesn't he or she have a responsibility to remain silent from the beginning? What does such a one really know about God that allows him or her to speak in an informed manner?

I say that unless a person can answer why an obviously capable God does not act in each instance to avert major moral outrages, then he or she cannot be certain that He acts to avert *any* moral outrages. On what basis could a person claim to know? I fear that inside the Christian family, we don't normally call ourselves to rational responsibility at this point. We have used the language so often in speaking to each other that we assume it makes sense. A reflective mind won't buy it.

Are you ready for the next step?

Let's assume that when God created man with finite freedom, He willingly placed certain limitations upon himself. And let's assume that with the creation of finite freedom comes the risk of evil. God cannot choose finite freedom for humankind and abolish the risks, or even the probability, of evil. He is therefore limited in what He can do if He wants also to retain finite freedom.

However, doesn't it seem that God should be able to do what a fireman can do? A fireman can rescue a child from a burning house as an exercise of freedom without damaging the moral and natural order. Can God be counted as all-good and all-powerful if He says to the child as she succumbs to the flames, "Sorry, but if I were to help you, I would introduce chaos into the relationship between finite freedom and the risks of freedom"?

Janice and Barbara, does it not seem strange that God can create a universe but can't rescue a child from a burning house? When finite firefighters rescue children, their moral and professional urgency is clear. They commit their skills and energies to saving each child if the rescue can be safely made. Does God expect more of a fireman than He does of himself?

At this point it is not unusual for presenters of the free will defense to say, "But God has a higher morality by which He acts. His ways are not our ways. They are incomprehensible. Hence, we must not call Him into question if He does not act according to our expectations."

But isn't it a strange "higher morality" that names as "good" what we are taught to name as "evil"? If one of us fails to assist in a crisis when we have the resources to do so, we will be judged immoral and irresponsible. We might even go to jail. Can God's "higher morality" have any meaning for us? Can we adopt for ourselves the excuses we allow for Him?

Are you still running with me?

Someone writing under the pen name B. C. Johnson has presented another intriguing critique of the free will defense. B. C. notes that the free will defense could just as easily support the existence of an evil God. Stated this way, the argument starts by saying that God is all-powerful and "all-evil." Following the free will line, we would then say that He allows free will so that people can freely do evil things. Doing so would make us more truly evil than if we had no choice in the matter. If people could not freely do evil, then they would not be truly free. Natural disasters occur so that people will have opportunities to become more selfish and bitter. Many succeed.

True, many people misuse their freedom by choosing to do good rather than evil.

However, their abuse of freedom in no way counts against the character of the evil God who gave us freedom to do either evil or good. Even though some persons choose the good, such an outcome is almost inevitable in order to protect freedom.

"But that's ridiculous," someone might say. Is it? Where is the flaw in B. C.'s argument? His idea isn't ridiculous just because we might not like what he is saying. What must one do to prove him wrong? If to do so one appeals to the Bible for support, then at least the free will defense can't claim to stand alone as a rationally compelling argument.

Janice and Barbara, somewhere along here, advocates of the free will defense usually make a major shift. Having recognized weaknesses in the argument, they implicitly step away from the present temporal order and into the future. Few people seem to be willing to say that evil is just pointless. They will not say that finally God must shrug His shoulders in evil's presence and say, "Well, I've done about all I can. Too bad."

Instead, they admit there is much we don't presently understand. True, there do appear to be some weaknesses in the free will defense. And yes, when watching rescue workers carry body bags away from the wreckage of some terrorists' crime, it does seem that the price paid for human freedom is too high. Two innocent children, strapped into their seats, slowly drown after their mother intentionally rolls her automobile into a South Carolina lake. Or, in 115-degree heat, a mother's two small children in McMinnville, Tennessee, suffocate in the mother's sweltering car. Where was the mother? Partying with four men in a motel room. Yes, at times it does appear that the unjust distribution of consequences from misused freedom challenge God's love and power.

However, defenders usually say to draw negative conclusions about God based on individual tragedies is immensely shortsighted. It is premature and highly selective. Our limited perspectives form a poor basis for questioning His omnipotence and goodness. Anyway, we should concentrate on all of the goodness in the world.

Even now, God is weaving a greater harmony that will one day be complete. When He has finished His plan, all evil will have been eliminated. Justice will reign. And much of what we once experienced as evil will be redeemed. The all-powerful and all-loving God will be vindicated before all people e and nations. Only then will we see the comprehensive goodness and beauty that He has been creating all along. Those who have been faithful to Him, who have worshiped and loved Him, will be vindicated.

The kingdom of God has not yet come in its fullness. But have no doubt—it will. He will finish the beautiful carpet He is weaving. Then we will see that He does all things well.

Long before that time, though, if we are perceptive, we can now catch beautiful glimpses of the divine Weaver at work. No matter how much the September 11 New York City attack seemed to count against God, there were plenty of indicators that an all-powerful, all-loving God was at work. Even through that horrible evil He was weaving a multicolored cosmic harmony. By early November, free will defenders would remind us, compassionate people had sent over one billion in donations to assist the families of the victims of the explosion. Much of the money was raised through bake sales, car washes, children sending in their pennies, and so on. Can anyone doubt that such acts of compassion prove that in spite of the immense evil in the world, God is putting in place an ultimate harmony?

When God's work is finished, all creation will know beyond question that the price paid for human freedom was well worth it!

As you may recall, Dostoyevsky placed this response on the lips of one of his characters in *The Brothers Karamazov*. The section of the book is "Rebellion." You remember Alyosha, the young Russian Orthodox seminarian who was a student of Father Zossima. And you remember his brother Ivan, who had major doubts about Christianity.

Barbara, I am reluctant to use this story because of your superior understanding of Dostoyevsky. But be patient with this novice. I consider Dostoyevsky an astute observer of humankind and of human evil.

At one point the two brothers are debating the problem of evil. Specifically, they are discussing the suffering of children. Ivan thinks that the innocent children should not suffer just because in "disgusting" ways adults choose to abuse their freedom. One of Alyosha's defenses is to admit that there is much that seems to contradict God's power and goodness. However, such observations are premature. God is now constructing a cosmic harmony. That harmony will prove that the cost in terms of human suffering was well worth the price for human freedom.

In the face of Alyosha's defense, Ivan tells some stories. He tells of a little girl of five who was hated by her mother and father. They were respectable people with a good education and breeding. These respectable parents subjected the child to all sorts of torture—beatings, kickings. Then they went to greater lengths. They smeared human excrement in the child's mouth and shut her up all night in the cold and frost of an outdoor privy. "Can you understand why a little creature, who can't even understand what's done to her, should beat her little aching heart with her little tiny fist in the dark and the cold, and weep her deep unresentful tears to dear, kind God to protect her?" Ivan drills his questions home: "Do you understand why this infamy must be and is permitted? Without it, I am told, man could not have existed on earth, for he could not have known good and evil. . . . Why, the whole world of knowledge is not worth that child's prayer to "dear, kind God'!"

Next, Ivan tells of an old retired Russian general who owned an estate of 2,000 serfs. He had kennels of hundreds of hounds and nearly a hundred dog handlers, all dressed in uniform. One day an eight-year-old boy threw a stone and accidentally injured a paw of the general's favorite hound. Seeing the hound limp, the old man demanded to know the reason. The child's act was exposed, and the general was furious.

He demanded that the boy be taken from his mother and shut up in a coop all night long. Early the next morning, the boy was brought into the old man's presence. The old man sat on his hunting horse. His hunting hounds had been prepared for the hunt. In the presence of the boy's mother and the servants, the child was brought from lockup and stripped naked. The child shivered with terror.

"Make him run," commanded the general. Then the child was forced to run, run like a fox.

When the boy had reached a sporting distance, the general yelled, "At him," and he set the whole pack of hounds on the child. The hounds caught the child and tore him to pieces before his mother's eyes.

The general was afterward declared incapable of administering his estates.

Lamely, Alyosha tries to answer that someday we will see that the "eternal harmony" God is designing is greater than the horrors Ivan has just described. Then Ivan will see that God has been vindicated. Ivan will "be there when everyone suddenly understands what it has all been for." Then he will know for certain that God should be worshiped and loved. Furthermore, to us God has given a ticket that invites us to participate in creating universal harmony.

But what of the children? Ivan asks. What am I to do about them?

"Listen! If all must suffer to pay for the eternal harmony, what have children to do with it, tell me please? . . . Why should they suffer, and why should they pay for the harmony?"

Ivan hastens to renounce a "higher harmony. It's not worth the tears of that one tortured five-year-old child who beat her chest and cried to 'dear, kind God.'"

Janice and Barbara, at this point Ivan asks a question that I want you to ask of yourselves. I have asked the question of myself many times and have never arrived at a satisfactory answer. For the free will defense to succeed as a coherent argument, at least one of you must be willing to answer a firm, conviction-filled "Yes!" I am going to raise Ivan's question and then close my letter. After you have read my letter carefully, respond to Ivan's question.

"Imagine that you are God attempting to create the eternal harmony with the object of making all men happy in the end," Ivan asks his brother. "What if in order to establish eternal harmony the only price you would have to pay would be the torture of that one little girl beating her breast with her fist, mouth smeared with excrement, and calling out in vain to 'dear, kind God'? Tell me, and tell me the truth, would you consent to be an architect [of eternal harmony] on those conditions?"

"No, I wouldn't consent," Alyosha said softly.

Would either of you consent?

Ivan also asks, "If men were to learn that the price of their harmony and happiness was the price of one little girl, could they remain happy forever?"

Ivan concludes, "I hasten to give back my entrance ticket . . . as soon as possible. I most respectfully return the ticket to God. Too high a price is asked for harmony." How can one worship and love a God who was willing to pay this price?

Janice and Barbara, don't answer quickly.

May Christ's love be yours in abundance,

Uncle Carl

14

Sunday, December 30, 2001
New York City

Dear Uncle Carl,

Your December 12 letter reached New York City on Monday, the 17th. The post office has said that monitoring for the presence of anthrax in the mail might slow delivery. Until now I really hadn't noticed any delay. But I suppose that with the crush of Christmas mail hitting the system, it's all just too much on the postal system.

I think that I did a fair job of concentrating on the conference proceedings. But I must tell you that your question, or more correctly, Ivan's question, has haunted me night and day. I have, of course, read *The Brothers Karamazov*. But never has Ivan's question struck me so forcefully. Janice has had much the same response.

Uncle Carl, your letter has thrown both of us into something of a tailspin. Admittedly, when I first began to raise Janice's questions with you, I told you that she would expect brutal honesty. But neither she nor I thought that a satisfactory solution to the problem of evil would be so difficult to achieve. We thought that at first you would clear away superficial answers. Then we assumed honest and satisfactory answers would emerge. Obviously, so far, this has not happened. We assume that you still have something up your sleeve.

We really expected that with minor adjustments, you would show the dependability of the free will defense. We had no idea that, as you have shown, the argument cannot muster sufficient rational support. Both of us now agree that it cannot stand as a satisfactory solution.

And then came Ivan's question.

Janice and I feel as though we are playing checkers and that each anticipated move has been blocked. We think that what we have to say in response to Ivan will apply as much to soul-making as to the free will defense.

At the outset, let us answer Ivan's second question. No, emphatically, no! We could not eternally enjoy a harmony whose cost was "no more" than the torture of one five-year-old, not to mention the eight-year-old child torn apart by the dogs.

Our first impulse was to try to work around Ivan. We planned to answer Ivan's question by saying God could not possibly have known humankind would so grossly abuse finite freedom. We were going to say that God "didn't see it coming." Nevertheless, after the Fall, God responded by acting redemptively. We were going to say that the universal harmony God is building in spite of evil should therefore prompt in us grateful worship and love, not blame. If this had been our response, then we could have given a "yes" to Ivan's question.

But we abandoned the idea. You have shown the weakness of saying that God created but could not have known humankind would abuse finite freedom.

Then we thought of arguing that God knew only a high likelihood, not certainty, that humankind would abuse its freedom. Hence, God is not at all to blame for evil.

However, we decided that this also is a faulty response to Ivan. We used the analogy of a corporation that knowingly produces a factory that has a high likelihood of damaging a populace. Under established standards of prosecution, the company would be liable for injuries to persons and property. This was true of Union Carbide. You may recall that in Bhopal, India, in 1984, some 6,600 people died when a poison cloud from Carbide's pesticide factory spread over the town. Union Carbide settled out of court for $470 million. It seems to us that a similar standard would apply to the divine Creator who gave freedom to humankind.

So it seems to us that selecting this path as a way to answer Ivan won't work either. We don't see how God could escape some responsibility for evil. As you pointed out in an earlier letter, if God is to some extent to blame for evil, then He is not all-good.

After abandoning those options, we toyed with the idea of just meeting Ivan's question head-on. We would just answer with a bold "Yes!" Yes, the excellence of the universal harmony and beauty God is creating, even in the midst of evil, is worth the price. We would knowingly allow the five-year-old girl to be locked up all night in a cold outdoor privy, her face smeared with excrement, praying fruitlessly to "dear, kind God." After all, her misery would last for only one cold night. Who knows? Maybe afterward the parents would come to their senses.

Uncle Carl, pursuit of that option stopped rather quickly. We could not seriously embrace it. Unless Janice and I are willing to abandon moral responsibility, we cannot answer "Yes." A morally responsible person will not knowingly permit torture of a child if he or she can prevent it. No measure of "harmony" could ever justify such an immoral choice. Besides, if we were to approve the little girl's torture, we would be engaging in the very thing harmony is supposed to eliminate. How can we arrive at harmony by adding to evil?

Claiming that universal harmony will be well worth the price paid in the coinage of man's abuse of freedom is morally and logically contradictory. Knowingly permitting evil, and vigorously promoting harmony, are mutually exclusive concepts. If not, then neither judges nor juries would have legitimate cause to punish a criminal.

If we were to give a "Yes" to Ivan's question, we would trivialize the child's value as a person. We would also trivialize morality, and we would make harmony pointless.

Uncle Carl, we cannot answer "Yes." And we don't see how any morally responsible person could either.

However, to answer "No" is equally unattractive. If we were to answer "No," we would indict God himself. We would have refused to do what the free will defense claims God was willing to do. We can't shrink from the conclusion: such a God would be our moral inferior.

If we try to avoid that conclusion by saying that God's morality is simply higher and wiser than ours, then we are bound to fall silent. The fundamental moral difference that seems to have opened between God and us leaves no basis for speech.

There seems to be one more option. We can admit that God is simply beyond our moral comprehension. Our knowledge of how He acts is negligible. And the questions about Him posed by evil cannot be satisfactorily answered. Nevertheless, we must love and worship Him anyway, just because He is God.

Uncle Carl, if this is where we must land, then for us the Christian faith loses its appeal and significance.

Painfully, we understand our predicament. We are unwilling to blame God for evil. But we seem to have no moral or rational basis for justifying our refusal.

Last evening Janice and I cooked dinner for Jeff. Then we showed him your letter and our response. We should have saved the food! Jeff studied the letters, smiled, and advised us to write another letter. We had already planned to do that. We didn't need his suggestion.

No doubt you have a satisfactory solution. Janice and I think it's time for you to deliver!

Waiting,
Barbara

15

Monday, January 7, 2002
Charleston, South Carolina

Dear Barbara,

Happy new year! I have anxiously awaited your letter. It arrived two days ago. Would you believe I skipped a fishing trip on Tuesday in hopes of receiving it? As much as I love receiving the Christmas cards from family and friends of long ago, I have much more been looking forward to the gift of your letter.

Barbara, you and Janice are to be complimented for the way you answered Ivan. Obviously, you arrived at your responses carefully and painfully. You addressed the major options and arrived where I believe the free will defense will likely lead an honest inquirer.

Barbara, I have nothing up my sleeve. I have wrestled with the problem of evil for many years. Even now, I know of no rationally coherent solution to the problem of evil. I don't believe there is one. No defense finally commends itself to a morally responsible person who wants to maintain belief in God as all-powerful and all-loving.

I am now counting the weeks until you, Janice, Michelle, and Tony come to Charleston. Although it is still two months away I am planning your itinerary.

Love,
Uncle Carl

16

Sunday, January 13, 2002
New York City

Dear Uncle Carl,

I'll not take long to write this letter. I am now in the rush of preparing for the beginning of spring semester. Janice is receiving much help from her counseling sessions. But in working through the grief process, she has a long way to go.

Uncle Carl, honestly, your January 7 letter shocked us. First, thank you for the compliment. But we find it hard to believe that you have no solutions. I must tell you that your letter caused no small amount of distress for Janice and for me. Frankly, we were quite disappointed in your lack of resources.

Neither could we understand why your letter ended so abruptly.

At least for Janice's sake, isn't there anything more to say? Her crisis of faith has deepened.

His peace be upon you,
Barbara

17

Sunday, January 20, 2002
Charleston, South Carolina

Dear Barbara and Janice,

This letter is for both of you.

Now there are just two months before you fly to Charleston. I long to see you.

I wish that you could be here tomorrow to go with me to the Dress Parade at the Citadel. I can't wait.

Well, my January 7 letter had the impact on the two of you I intended: frustration (and did I detect a little bit of anger from my lovable niece?).

Can I say more? Yes. But it won't come through rational or philosophical argument. As helpful as such aids may be, they are of very limited assistance to the Christian faith. Even the most fruitful rational "answers" come to a stop quite short of the station.

I admit that I have led you through a rather demanding and frustrating process. There are reasons. Some of the defenses do have some limited value for Christians. But there is a more important reason.

Paul Tillich, a theologian, wrote a book titled *The Shaking of the Foundations*. The title comes from Heb. 12:26-28, which speaks of God shaking all that can be shaken so that only what cannot be shaken will remain. Christ and the kingdom of God cannot be shaken.

Too often, when dealing with the problem of evil, Christians stand on shakable ground. For "solutions" they grasp at what eventually shakes and tumbles. Too many flimsy statements pass as satisfactory Christian answers for the problem of evil.

I have deliberately taken you through the shaking process. I want you to stand where Christians ought to stand: in the cross and resurrection of Jesus Christ.

The Christian faith has no adequate rational "justification" or "solution" for the problem of evil. But it does have a more-than-adequate response.

Christian faith. What does this mean? It means in part that everything that can be said or believed about God must be evaluated in light of the person and work of Jesus Christ. "He who has seen me has seen the Father" (John 14:9). "No one has ever seen God; the only Son, who is in the bosom of the Father, he has made him known" (1:18).

All questions about God, the world, and evil must be submitted to God's self-disclosure in Jesus. In Christ, God's revelation of himself is so complete, so redemptive, and so full of peace and hope that all challenges regarding God's character and authority assume secondary significance.

For a response to the reality of evil, the Christian faith turns to the cross and resurrection of Jesus Christ. After Alyosha had struggled to answer Ivan's question, Ivan asked him why he had not begun with the crucified Christ.

In the Cross, God answers forever all questions regarding His goodness. On Easter morning, God settles all questions regarding His sovereignty. No matter how troubling the questions regarding evil, Christians should look to the Cross and Resurrection.

When we Christians turn to the cross and resurrection of Jesus, the questions do not cease to be painful and difficult. They don't go away. In fact, as we shall see, the questions will likely become even more painful. "The angry cry of protest against evil," theologian Jurgen Moltmann said, "is sustained by man's longing for the One who is completely different." If God is not who the Christian faith claims Him to be, if He is less, then the protest against evil tends to lose its moral and intellectual force. Allow me to slightly paraphrase a statement by Moltmann I used weeks ago: "The sting in the question 'Why is there suffering?' is God. And the sting in the question 'Is there a God?' is suffering."

What sort of God do we meet in the Cross? None other than the God who suffers with us. The Cross guarantees that God is present with us. He doesn't stand safely aloof. In Christ we meet the eternal God, who so radically identifies with a suffering world that He takes the world's evil upon himself. Not just the sins of the world, but the unfathomable abyss of evil. In Christ, God radically identifies with human brokenness. He suffers the heinous death of His only begotten Son.

How extensively does God suffer? Well, what did the Cross symbolize for the Romans? The ultimate in vulnerability, human suffering, humiliation, rejection, and loneliness. God became what we do not want to be—an outcast, accursed, crucified. The eternal God took all of this and more upon himself. He did it not because some external power imposed it on Him, but because in love God freely chose it! God did not die, but He exhaustively suffered the death of His Son.

God knows the bitterness of the human condition from the inside, from the bottom up. In this we catch a glimpse of the inner mystery of God.

A few years ago, the 18-year-old son of friends of mine died in his sleep. The grief-stricken parents told me that in their grief they entered a dark and lonely valley. Even the words of the Bible could not comfort them there. While in that valley, Jesus' cry on the Cross, "My God, my God, why hast thou forsaken me?" (Matt. 27:46), became their point of contact with God. From the human side, they were expressing the meaning of God's radical identity with suffering. He became, and continues to be, one with us! Even Jesus' astonishing words while on the Cross express confidence in the Heavenly Father's faithfulness. Jesus was quoting from Ps. 22, which concludes in a hymn of worship and confidence in God's presence and deliverance.

The cross of Christ is either the end of all hope, or it is the beginning of a specifically Christian hope. When we Christians talk about evil, we should speak while gazing upon the One who was crucified and abandoned on the Cross. There we encounter the pathos [suffering and compassion] of God.

Janice and Barbara, God's suffering in His Son on the Cross reveals the way He is affected by suffering in the world. The creation is His, and He suffers radically and freely with it. This is how seriously He takes the creation.

The apostle Paul compares God's sufferings with the world to a mother's labor pains during childbirth. He says that the creation is "groaning in travail" and that the Holy Spirit groans, or travails, with it. As Paul sees it, these are sufferings of hope or in hope. They are accompanied by expectation, not by despair (Rom. 8:22-27). God suffers with the creation in order to redeem it. He is bringing forth a new creation through Christ Jesus (2 Cor. 5:17-19; Rev. 21:1).

God does more than suffer with us on the Cross. He suffers under the actions of man, even the death of Jesus. God's sufferings in Christ are the supreme verification of His covenantal relation with us. There He fulfills His promises to the world and demonstrates without doubt that He is all-loving (John 10:11-15; Rom. 5:6-8).

The Cross is not the only place we learn of the God who suffers with us, but it is the supreme place of God's self-emptying pathos, His self-imposed vulnerability.

Barbara and Janice, this is the Christian gospel. It is the focus of Christian faith. The only ones who can seriously question whether God is all-loving are those who do not understand the gospel of the Cross. Eternally, the Cross establishes the inexhaustible goodness of God.

But what about God's omnipotence? Maybe although what Christians say about God's goodness is true, He is not omnipotent. To this idea the Christian faith responds with an unqualified "No!" What the New Testament affirms regarding God's goodness, it just as thoroughly affirms regarding His sovereignty. How do we know that God is all-powerful? The answer is absolutely central to the gospel and the New Testament: the resurrection of Jesus on Easter morning. Supremely, God demonstrated His sovereignty by raising His Son from the dead (Gal. 1:1; Eph. 1:20).

On Easter, God answers the Son's question on the Cross, "Have you forsaken me?" Jesus' question was asked on behalf of all the members of Adam's race. Does suffering—even redemptive suffering—have the final word? Is love finally overwhelmed by evil? Is it finally impotent, joined to a loving but finite God? The apostle Paul squarely faced the power of these questions and did not retreat from their implications. If divine love is alone, then finally, all is vanity (1 Cor. 15:14).

Easter is God's eternal answer to those questions. Easter means that unquestionably and inseparably, love and sovereignty are joined (2 Cor. 13:4). In Christ's resurrection, the Father shows that His "abandonment" of the Son on the Cross had nothing to do with desertion or powerlessness in the presence of evil.

Instead, the holy God turned His back on sin but not on His Son. God's "turning" discloses even more clearly just how thoroughly the Son suffered for a sinful and broken world. He identified with us at depths the holy God could not look upon. Any parent who has ever suffered with a child knows that parental suffering increases along with the child's. Janice and Barbara, I will tell you something I don't fully understand. The Father's abandonment of His Son is the other side of His radical identification with Him and with this broken world.

When the worst that evil could do—crucify the Son of God—had been done, it still was not enough to establish evil's authority. Evil could not keep Jesus in the grave. Easter declares that God is sovereign and that evil is finite and temporary. As Christians we live in hope and confidence that the God of Holy Love who inaugurated His kingdom in Christ Jesus will bring it to completion. That is why Christians through the centuries have prayed *Maranatha!* "Our Lord, come!" (1 Cor. 15:24; 16:22).

Janice and Barbara, the New Testament leaves no doubt about this. The apostle Paul told the Ephesian Christians that the same power by which God raised Jesus from the dead is the power that is now at work in the children of God. We Christians live in the message of the Cross and by the power of Jesus' resurrection:

I want you to know about the great and mighty power that God has for us followers. It is the same wonderful power he used when he raised Christ from death and let him sit at his right side in heaven. There Christ rules over all forces, authorities, powers, and rulers. He rules over all beings in this world and will rule in the future world as well. God has put all things under the power of Christ, and for the good of the church he has made him the head of everything (1:19-22, CEV).

That, Janice and Barbara, is the omnipotence of God. It is displayed in the resurrection and ascension of Jesus Christ, not in philosophical debate.

Now, Janice and Barbara, each day is Easter. In all places and circumstances—including New York City—let the word go out. In Christ, suffering love and omnipotence are joined, never to be separated. The one confirms the other. "But God, who is rich in mercy, out of the great love with which he loved us, even when we were dead through our trespasses, made us alive together with Christ (by grace you have been saved), and raised us up with him, and made us sit with him in the heavenly places in Christ Jesus" (Eph. 2:4-6).

Do the cross and resurrection of Christ tell us why there is evil in the world? No. They do not. I said earlier that for Christians the problem of evil becomes even more intense. However, the cross and resurrection of Christ do place final brackets or boundaries around evil. The evil inside the brackets does not disappear or become less intense. However, because of the Cross and Resurrection, evil forfeits its claim to authority and finality. The apostle Paul says that God has "disarmed the principalities and powers and made a public example of them, triumphing over them in him" (Col. 2:15). Evil's sentence (Rom. 8:3) to humiliation and destruction has been delivered by the all-loving and all-powerful Father of our Lord.

Because this is true, Janice and Barbara, Christians live as hope-filled people. The gospel is a gospel of hope. Christian hope is grounded in faith in the God who suffered in His Son and who did not abandon Him to the grave.

Christian hope is not the same as optimism. Its basis is not the ups and downs and moods of the time. Hope's foundation is the God who has come and who will come. The early Christians prayed, "Marana tha—Come, O Lord!" (1 Cor. 16:22, NEB). They were praying for their Lord to complete the kingdom of God in which they were already living. Those early Christians lived in and toward hope. Today, through the Holy Spirit, Christ makes it possible for us to live in hope. Hope is a central meaning of the sacrament of the Lord's Supper.

Christian hope is confidence that the same God who suffered in His Son and raised Him from the grave will finish what He has begun. Hope is the substance of Christian existence in the Church and in the world.

In the Church and in the world. This is where Christians live out their hope. We bear witness to Christian hope by identifying with the sufferings of the world. I think this is partly what the apostle Paul meant when he spoke of wanting to know Christ "and the power of his resurrection and the fellowship of sharing in his sufferings" (Phil. 3:10, NIV). If Christ revealed God through the way He related to suffering, then as Christ's servants we are to do the same. By contrast, escapism, condemnation, and ease betray the gospel.

If Father Paneloux had been guided by Christian hope, he, not Dr. Rieux the humanist, would have been the first one in the streets. Christians who flee the plague, who think that God has abandoned the world to suffering, deny the meaning of the cross and resurrection of Christ.

J. Christiaan Beker, professor of biblical theology at Princeton Seminary, has helped me understand how Christian hope should be lived out in the world. He says that we Christians are now called "to bad things." "Christians are called to suffer redemptively in the world on behalf of their hope in God's coming kingdom of justice. Indeed, redemptive suffering on behalf of others is the signature of Christian hope in our idolatrous world. Hope that severs itself from suffering in and for the world ceases to be authentic Christian hope."

You have been very patient to read such a long letter. I want to close it with one of my favorite statements from the apostle Paul. As you know, he profoundly influenced the Church's understanding of Christian hope: "In all these things we are more than conquerors through him who loved us. For I am sure that neither death, nor life, nor angels, nor principalities, nor things present, nor things to come, nor powers, nor height, nor depth, nor anything else in all creation, will be able to separate us from the love of God in Christ Jesus our Lord" (Rom. 8:37-39).

May the One who raised Jesus from the grave establish the two of you in faith, hope, and love.

Uncle Carl

18

Thursday, January 31, 2002
New York City

Dear Uncle Carl,

Perhaps you have wondered when I would respond to your January 20 letter. I apologize for not answering earlier. The activities associated with beginning a new semester are in full swing here. My plans for beginning new classes never seem to be sufficient.

Janice and I have carefully read your letter three times. We have studied the scriptures to which you referred.

Uncle Carl, we simply did not anticipate the content of your letter. We were demanding more and better arguments. You called us to be disciples of Jesus Christ. I should have known you would move in this direction.

After all the letters, in an important sense, you have made evil more difficult than it was before for Janice and me. The pain has certainly not lessened. But you have shown us where we should stand.

Janice was deeply moved by your letter. She hasn't said much. As you would expect, she still has a long way to go in the grief process. But in response to your last letter, I think that I have observed the beginning of a transformation in her. After we had read your letter for the third time, she said, "Barbara, I think that I am beginning to see it. I think the direction I must take is becoming clearer." Those were cautious but deeply expressed words. If hope can be observed, I think that I am beginning to hear it in Janice's voice and see it on her face.

Uncle Carl, a question has surfaced. If the Cross and Resurrection are so pivotal in the Christian response to evil, why do so many Christians stand elsewhere? Doesn't it strike you as strange that the center of our faith would be pushed to the edges in favor of other responses?

In a few weeks, Janice and I will continue our conversation with you in Charleston. I think Janice is more excited about the trip than even I am.

Please write as soon as possible.

Your loving niece,
Barbara